RELIGION IS DYING

Soaring Secularism in America and the West

James A. Haught

For my new wife Nancy Lince, and for my writer-sister Helen Haught Fanick, who is smart enough to design books for publication.

Acknowledgements:

This book consists chiefly of published essays, mostly from *Free Inquiry* magazine.

Part of the assemblage was published in 2010 as *Fading Faith: The Rise of the Secular Age* by Gustav Broukal Press, an imprint of American Atheists.

The author is grateful to Broukal editors for their permission to revise and reissue the book, with a dozen new chapters added.

CONTENTS

PART ONE: CHURCH DECLINE

Chapter 1

FADING FAITH

The sea of faith

Was once, too, at the full, and round Earth's shore

Lay like the folds of a bright girdle furled

But now I only hear

Its melancholy, long, withdrawing roar,

Retreating....

- Matthew Arnold, Dover Beach

A historic transition is occurring, barely noticed. Slowly, quietly, imperceptibly, religion is shriveling in America, as it has done in Europe, Canada, Australia, Japan and other advanced societies. Supernatural faith increasingly belongs to the Third World. The First World is entering the long-predicted Secular Age, when science and knowledge dominate. The change promises to be another shift of civilization, like past departures of the era of kings, the time of slavery, the Agricultural Age, the epoch of colonialism, and the like. Such cultural transformations are partly invisible to contemporary people, but become obvious in retrospect.

Of course, religiosity remains huge in America. The retreat of belief is difficult to see amid boisterous megachurches of millionaire preachers. It's obscured by puritanical politics of white evangelicals. It's masked by around-the-clock television and radio evangelism, paid broadcasting competing commercially for market share. It's hidden by record-breaking sales of "Rapture" books, by attempts to undercut the teaching of evolution, by rapid growth of talking-in-tongues Pentecostals, and other fundamentalist ferment.

Yet America's religious decline advances, year after year, decade by decade, beneath the surface. Faith in invisible gods, devils, heavens, hells, angels, demons, virgin births, resurrections, miracles, messiahs, visions, prophecies, incarnations, reincarnations, spirit possessions, exorcisms, holy visitations, mystical revelations and other supernaturalism

1

silently is eroding among thinking Americans.

Evidence of church decay is visible in several ways: Polls show "none" to be the fastest-growing American religious choice, especially among the young. One-tenth of American adults now are lapsed Catholics, as twenty million have quit the church. Mainline Protestant denominations, once a bastion of the educated, have withered drastically, implying that the educated no longer need religion. Methodists have lost more than a thousand members a week for nearly fifty years. Church-rooted taboos that dominated America a half-century ago have vanished. Decline of seminarians has produced a clergy shortage in the Catholic Church, which has been forced to import Third World priests. The American populace trusts science and medicine for crucial decisions, not prayer and incantations. Successful politicians still must proclaim their piety and declare "God bless America," but most of society lives as if gods are absent. Secularism is taking control, even while television evangelists preside over hundred-million-dollar conglomerates.

THE SECULARIZATION THESIS

First, some background: For three centuries, scientific-minded skeptics have predicted that supernaturalism will die as human knowledge advances. Around 1700, Thomas Woolston and other British Enlightenment thinkers declared that Christianity would disappear within a couple of centuries.[1] Frederick the Great wrote to his doubting colleague Voltaire that faith swiftly was "crumbling of itself."[2]

Such assertions contradicted the culture of those times, because religion was so important to Europeans that they had spent centuries killing people for it - in Crusades against Muslims, witch hunts, Holy Inquisitions, pogroms against Jews, Catholic-Protestant wars of the Reformation, persecutions of Anabaptists, Hussite wars, extermination of "heretics," burning of nonconformists, and such faith-based slaughter. Blasphemy laws sent doubters (including Woolston) to prison.

As the Enlightenment spread to America, Deist-minded founding fathers joined the forecast. Thomas Jefferson privately wrote: "The day will come when the mystical generation of Jesus, by the supreme being as his father in the womb of a virgin, will be classed with the fable of the generation of Minerva in the brain of Jupiter."[3] And he wrote: "The priests of the different sects... dread the advance of science as witches do the approach of daylight."[4] And he predicted the end of Christianity by writing: "I trust there is not a young man now living in the United States who will not die a Unitarian."[5]

Back in Europe, French philosopher Auguste Comte wrote that humanity was outgrowing its primitive "theological stage." Frederich Engels boasted that the collectivist revolution would make religion evaporate. In 1878, Max Muller said:

"Every day, every week, every month, every quarter, the most widely read journals seem just now to vie with each other in telling us that the time for religion is past, that faith is a hallucination or an infantile disease, that the gods have at last been found out and exploded."[6]

As the twentieth century ensued, anthropologist A.E. Crawley wrote in 1905 that "the opinion is everywhere gaining ground that

3

religion is a mere survival from a primitive...age, and its extinction is only a matter of time."[7] Sigmund Freud and others said the neurotic fantasy soon would fade.

"Is Christianity dying?" Will Durant asked in 1961 in *The Age of Reason Begins*. He wondered if faith is "suffering slow decay through the spread of knowledge, the widening of astronomic, geographical, and historical horizons, the realization of evil in history and the soul, the decline of faith in an afterlife and of trust in the benevolent guidance of the world? If this is so, it is the basic event of modern times."

In 1966, University of Pennsylvania anthropologist Anthony F.C. Wallace wrote that "the evolutionary future of religion is extinction."[8] Famed Boston University sociologist Peter Berger told *The New York Times* that by "the twenty-first century, religious believers are likely to be found only in small sects, huddled together to resist a worldwide secular culture.... The predicament of the believer is increasingly like that of a Tibetan astrologer on a prolonged visit to an American university."[9]

By the 1960s, social scholars generally accepted the "secularization thesis"—that advancing education, prosperity, science and technology in highly developed nations spelled doom for otherworldly beliefs.

EUROPE'S FAITH FIZZLED

That thesis was accurate for Western Europe and several other advanced places. After World War II, European churchgoing suffered spectacular shrinkage. The continent where millions once were killed for religion abruptly

4

concluded that religion was of no importance. In Catholic France, fewer than seven percent of adults now attend worship.[10] Continent-wide, a Gallup Poll found that just fifteen percent go to church.[11] Attendance at European churches and cathedrals today consists mostly of a few old women, outnumbered by gawking tourists.

Pope Benedict XVI complained: "Europe has developed a culture that, in a manner unknown before now to humanity, excludes God from the public conscience." He protested the new European attitude of "disdaining God completely."[12] Newspaper columnist George Will called the Vatican "109 acres of faith in a European sea of unbelief."[13]

Nun-turned-historian Karen Armstrong says: "Copenhagen, Stockholm, London - these are the secular capitals of the world." Any Englishman who expresses faith in God is deemed "eccentric," she says.[14] When the European Union wrote a new continental constitution, it omitted any mention of God or Christianity, to the outrage of the church.

In Denmark and Sweden, fewer than five percent of adults are in church on a typical Sunday, Danish psychologist Lars Dencik wrote in 2006. "A good eighty percent of the population can be characterized as 'secular' in the sense that religious practices do not play any part in their daily life." He said Denmark's religious Christian-Democratic political party attracts only two percent of voters.[15]

Pitzer College sociologist Phil Zuckerman spent a year interviewing Scandinavians and wrote *Society Without God: What the Least-Religious Nations Can Tell Us About Contentment*. He asserts that irreligious Scandinavians are happier than residents of highly religious cultures. Dr. Zuckerman said:

"The notion that religious belief is childish, that earnest prayer is something only children engage in, and that faith in God is just something one dabbles with in childhood but eventually grows out of as one becomes a mature adult, would strike most Americans as offensive. But for millions of Scandinavians, that's just the way it is."

Once-Catholic Ireland is another example. Huge Irish churches today are mostly vacant, except for handfuls of aging women. The mighty Archdiocese of Dublin graduated only one priest in 2004, and ordained none in 2005. Priest Brendan Hoban, author of *Change or Decay: Irish Catholicism in Crisis*, lamented: "We are a modern and prosperous country, and many Catholics no longer find their faith useful." At Dublin's cavernous Most Precious Blood Church, priest Thomas McCarthy recalled a vanished time when four Sunday masses were packed: "There were fierce crowds coming back then. The message was clear: Come to mass or go to hell. Well, that doesn't work anymore."[16]

The world's lowest birthrate is in Catholic Italy. The church's ban on birth control doesn't work any better than its "come to mass or go to hell" warning.

More than half of British children attended Sunday school at the start of the twentieth century. By 2000, the rate was down to four percent.[17] A nationwide poll in 2000 by Ipsos-MORI asked British adults to name "inspirational" figures. Sixty-five percent picked Nelson Mandela, six percent chose Britney Spears, and one percent named Jesus.

Stuart Macdonald of the University of Toronto's Centre for Clergy Care described "the rapid secularization of Scotland," noting: "The Church of Scotland, which had the power to force its morality on the society to the extent that swings in public parks were chained up in the early 1960s in order that the sabbath be properly observed, is now invisible within Scottish society."[18]

Intense religion in Europe today is confined chiefly to Third World immigrants. Tropical newcomers to Britain attend tongues-talking Pentecostal assemblies. "Skins of other hues are increasingly evident in European churches," scholar Philip Jenkins wrote. "Half of all London churchgoers are now black."[19]

Much of the continent worries about Muslim immigrants who subjugate women and practice moralistic strictures. In 2004, France banned Muslim headscarves - along with Jewish skullcaps, Sikh turbans and other conspicuous religious garb - from public schools. Muslim rigidity upsets secular Europeans so much that outspoken atheist groups have sprung up in France and elsewhere to counter this growing intrusion into the laissez-faire culture.

OTHER SECULAR HOTSPOTS

The secularization thesis also proved correct in various other Western democracies:

In Canada, the national census records religious preference. Starting in the 1960s, a category of "no religion" was added. At first, only one percent of Canadian adults chose that label, but a remarkable upsurge happened. Today, around twenty percent choose it.

Canada's General Social Survey reported:

7

"Attendance at religious services has fallen dramatically across the country over the past 15 years. Nationally, only one-fifth of individuals aged 15 and over attended religious services on a weekly basis in 2001.... Four in ten adults (forty-three percent) reported that they had not attended religious services during the twelve months prior to the survey."

CanWest News Service reported that the Anglican Church of Canada lost more than half its members between 1961 and 2001 - and the United Church of Canada dropped thirty-nine percent - and the Presbyterian Church of Canada fell thirty-five percent. Ontario Consultants on Religious Tolerance reported that "self-professed atheists, agnostics, humanists, secularists and people of no religious adherence are increasing rapidly."[20]

In Australia, nineteen percent of adults replied "no religion" in the 2006 census, and twelve percent more wouldn't answer, which indicates that nearly a third of Australians have become secular. Church attendance is much lower. The Australian Community Survey says forty-five percent of Australians were regular worshipers in 1950, but only twenty percent were in 2000.

As a prank, some irreverent young Australians launched a "Jedi" religion spoof. Through a flood of e-mails, they urged fellow conspirators around the world to list their faith as Jedi ("May the Force be with you") in national censuses. Chris Brennan, president of the Australian Star Wars Appreciation Society, told news reporters it was a massive practical joke. In the 2001 census, more than 70,000 Australians named Jedi as their religion. In neighboring New Zealand, 53,000 did. The craze had its largest effect in England and Wales, where 390,127 claimed Jedi faith in the 2001 census. Scotland added 14,052 more.

Meanwhile, New Zealand is even more secular than Australia. Around forty percent of New Zealand adults reply "no religion" or refuse to answer when questioned in censuses. This group has grown to be the largest segment in the beliefs category of the census.

Japan sometimes is called the world's most secular society. Although a vague sense of Shinto spirit-worship and godless Buddhism lingers from the past - rather like secular Americans celebrating Christmas - few Japanese today attend temples to worship. A 2000 survey by *Yomiuri Shimbun* newspaper found that three-fourths call themselves nonbelievers - although the paper's first religion survey in 1952 had found only one-third lacking belief.[21] A Japan-Guide poll asked "Are you religious?" and got this response: sixteen percent "yes," eighty-four percent "no" or "don't know."

Several cult-like "new religions" arose in Japan, including Aum Shinrikyo (Supreme Truth), whose followers murdered critics and planted homemade nerve gas in Tokyo's subways in 1995, killing a dozen commuters and sickening a thousand. InfoJapan says many young Japanese are leery of faith because of the Aum tragedy and the role that Shinto played in pulling the island nation into World War II.

In the Jewish nation of Israel, most Jews aren't Jews by religion. A 2004 survey found that almost two-thirds of the country's European-ancestry Jews are nonobservant. The ratio of seculars soars among the well-

9

educated and affluent. "Israel's intellectual, literary, scientific and artistic elite is overwhelmingly nonobservant," Dr. Benjamin Beit-Hallahmi, a University of Haifa psychologist, wrote. He added that no prime ministers except Menachem Begin attended synagogues, outside of government ceremonies. However, Israeli Jews from Third World nations are much more religious.[22] Tellingly, the psychologist wrote:

"Religiosity among Israeli Jews is correlated with hawkishness and conservatism, paralleling findings reported all over the world." He said 85 percent of ultra-Orthodox Israeli Jews oppose releasing the occupied West Bank for a Palestinian homeland - but only 17 percent of secular Israelis do.[23]

Similarly, a 2009 Pew Forum survey of American adults found that nearly two-thirds of white evangelicals support torturing Muslim terror suspects, but only forty percent of unchurched Americans do.[24]

AMERICA'S IMMENSE RELIGIOSITY

The United States has been a major exception that seemed to discredit the secularization thesis. America, the most technologically advanced and prosperous of all nations, remained as religious as any impoverished Third World land. The United States has 350,000 churches whose members donate $100 billion per year. Polls often find Americans' belief in God, heaven, hell, angels and the like around 90 percent, far above findings in the rest of the West. American churchgoing likewise is much higher. Puritanical white fundamentalists and evangelicals became the conservative bedrock of the Republican Party, endlessly seeking to outlaw abortions, ostracize gays, obstruct teaching of evolution, restore school prayer, install governmental religious displays, increase the death penalty, support pistol-carrying, and the like. A 2004 *Newsweek* survey found that four-fifths of Americans think Jesus was born of a virgin, without a human father, and more than half think Jesus will return to Earth.

American evangelism is a teeming industry of one-man denominations, all competing for bigger market shares. Charismatic preachers draw followers who give money to buy radio and television time, which enables the ministers to reach ever-bigger audiences, which give ever-bigger sums, which buy more airtime, ad infinitum. Successful entrepreneurs start small, and then grow to the limit of their exhortation skills, or until scandal scuttles them. The Rev. Pat Robertson's Christian Broadcasting Network swelled to a $240-million-per-year empire with many religious subsidiaries (despite Robertson's proclivity for goofy remarks and claims). The Rev. James Dobson's Focus on the Family rose to a $150 million budget - and Republican presidential candidates groveled for Dobson's endorsement - but in 2008 he suffered a financial setback and laid off 200 employees.

"Bishop" T.D. Jakes was an impoverished West Virginian living on welfare, until he discovered his evangelist charisma and rose to luxury. Now he wears huge diamonds, travels by private jet, occupies mansions and lives like a king. Sale of evangelist books, videos, audiotapes and CDs became a billion-dollar industry, enriching religious entrepreneurs.

Commercialization of faith rose so severely

that Senator Chuck Grassley, Republican of Iowa, launched congressional hearings in 2007 into "prosperity gospel" preachers who reap enormous fortunes. But fellow Republicans feared damage to the party's most loyal core. President George W. Bush's liaison to evangelicals, Doug Wead, said: "Grassley has thrown a grenade in the middle of the coalition that any Republican will need. If you are a Republican, it looks disastrous."[25]

Bible prophecy is a large segment of American fundamentalism. Evangelist Tim LaHaye and writing partner Jerry Jenkins set astounding sales records for their *Left Behind* novels describing the Rapture, when Jesus returns to wreak gory vengeance upon everyone except born-again Christians. The books describe Christ casting billions of Hindus, Muslims, Buddhists, Jews, Catholics, Unitarians, secular people and others into hell. "Jesus merely raised one hand a few inches and...they tumbled in, howling and screeching," one novel says. The flesh of non-Christians dissolves from their skeletons. The *Left Behind* series passed 60 million sales, becoming America's most lucrative book venture, outselling all works, even the best writing of Nobel and Pulitzer prizewinners. Altogether, evangelical books are nearly a $2 billion market in America.

Pentecostals who "speak in tongues" are growing. During the 1990s, the Pentecostal Assemblies of God leaped eighteen percent in America, to become larger than the dying Episcopal Church. Mormons - the unusual sect based on mysterious golden plates that an angel reportedly revealed, then took back - keep rising in membership to nearly six million in America, despite lingering disputes over the

12

fringe practice of polygamy.

University of Cincinnati political scientist George Bishop found that forty-five percent of Americans reject evolution and accept divine creation, but just seven percent of Britons do, and even fewer in Germany, Norway, Russia and the Netherlands.[26]

"One of the most interesting puzzles in the sociology of religion," Boston University's Berger wrote, "is why Americans are so much more churchly than Europeans."[27] Because of America's churchliness, Dr. Berger, a lifelong Lutheran, publicly reversed his past endorsement of the secularization thesis. Other scholars, especially Dr. Rodney Stark of Southern Baptist Baylor University and Catholic philosopher Charles Taylor, led an academic revolt, saying previous researchers were wrong when they predicted the demise of faith.

A scholar battle ensued. Scottish sociologist Steve Bruce wrote *God is Dead: Secularization in the West*, contending that the ongoing decay of religion is overwhelmingly evident in the First World, and irreversible. Dr. Bruce attributes secularism not to rising science but to growing relativism: People see the world's kaleidoscope of conflicting supernatural systems and begin to question whether any is true. "The greatest damage to religion has been caused," he wrote, "not by competing secular ideas, but by the general relativism that supposes all ideologies are equally true (and hence equally false)."

Much of Bruce's work focuses on Britain, where he predicts that Methodism will vanish within a generation and the Church of England will dwindle to "a trivial voluntary association with a large portfolio of heritage property." But

13

he also sees America belatedly following the same relentless course. He says there's clear evidence that Christianity is losing power, prestige and popularity in the United States, consistent with the "secularization paradigm." For example, he notes that the "new Christian Right," the political alliance between white evangelicals and the Republican Party, failed to achieve the impact on American society that was expected in the 1970s.

RISING AMERICAN 'NONES'

Well, it turns out that the scholars who decided they had been wrong about secularization were wrong in saying they had been wrong. New trends show secularism growing rapidly in America, even amid booming piety. While the nation's religious extravaganza fills revival channels and enters the daily news, an erosion of faith surreptitiously is snowballing, mostly out of sight, barely noticed.

Evidence keeps accumulating, as follows:

Since 1990, surveys indicate that the godless ratio in America doubled from one-tenth to one-fifth of the adult population, a swift transformation. The 2008 American Religious Identification Survey by researchers at Trinity College, Hartford, Connecticut, found that fifteen percent - thirty-four million adults - gave their religion as "none." Another five percent - twelve million - answered "don't know" or refused to reply, which is interpreted to rank with the "nones." Thus, around forty-five million American adults evidently live apart from churchgoing. This number has skyrocketed since the first ARIS poll in 1990, which found eight percent "nones."

The 2008 survey concluded that the share of Americans who call themselves Christians fell ten percent since 1990, from eighty-six percent to seventy-six. Nearly all this loss came from traditional Protestant "mainline" faiths with university-educated clergy. There was significant growth in fundamentalists, evangelicals, Pentecostals, and Mormons, the off-brand Christians who believe that Jesus visited an ancient American civilization.

"There is a real and growing theological polarization in American society whereby thirty-four percent of the population believe they are 'born again' but twenty-five to thirty percent reject the idea of a personal divinity," the ARIS report said in a section about convictions. "These questions on belief reveal the cultural polarization between the pious and nonreligious portions of the national population, which are today roughly similar in size."

ARIS researcher Ariela Keysar told Catholic News Agency: "The Nones are the only group to have grown in every state of the union." She said American nonbelievers were stigmatized in the past, but the social climate has shifted, so that they feel "more free to step forward, less looked upon as outcasts." ARIS director Mark Silk added: "You're not declaring yourself a total pariah. The culture has changed in a way that makes it easier to say, 'No, I don't have a religion.'"

Their report added: "The challenge to Christianity in the United States does not come from other religions but rather from a rejection of all forms of organized religion."

Significantly, males predominate among America's soaring "nones," which matches

15

international findings that females are more churchly. The ARIS report said: "The most gender-unbalanced group is the Nones, those who profess no religion or self-identified as atheists or agnostics. The ratio of sixty males to forty females is a remarkable result. These gender patterns correspond with many earlier findings that show women to be more religious than men."

American Catholics slid only a bit in the new ARIS study, from twenty-six percent of the adult population to twenty-five percent. Jewish synagogue and temple worship faded slightly. "The Jewish population is in slow decline due mainly to a movement toward the Nones among young ethnic Jews," the report added. "This is part of a general trend among younger white Americans." The number of American Muslims nearly tripled, to 1.3 million, but they remain less than one percent of the adult population.

Since a second ARIS survey in 2001, dramatic change occurred in New England. "The decline of Catholicism in the Northeast is nothing short of stunning," chief researcher Barry Kosmin told Catholic News Agency. The ARIS report added: "New England had a net loss of one million Catholics." They fell from forty-six percent of the region's adult population to thirty-six percent. Other northeastern churches also declined. Southern Baptist Theological Seminary President Albert Mohler told *Newsweek*: "To lose New England struck me as momentous.... Clearly, there is a new narrative, a post-Christian narrative, that is animating large portions of this society."[28]

Meanwhile, a 2008 United States Religious Landscape Survey by the Pew Forum on Religion and Public Life found even more

16

dramatic results. It ranked "nones" as America's second-largest adult group, after Catholics. Its report said twenty-four percent identify themselves as Roman Catholic, sixteen percent have no religion, and the third-biggest segment was "evangelical Baptist" at eleven percent.

Pew findings about Catholicism were a jolt. The report said more than twenty million American Catholics have quit the church, thus one-tenth of American adults now are ex-Catholics. The denomination would have lost one-third of its membership, Pew concluded, except for a flood of Hispanic immigrants who offset the outflow. Phil Lawler, author of *The Faithful Departed*, wrote for Catholic World News:

"The most important story about Catholicism in America over the course of the past generation has not been the sex-abuse scandal, nor the changes that followed Vatican II. The most important story is the vast exodus of Catholics leaving the faith."

James Davidson of The Catholic University of America lamented that many American Catholics "seem increasingly indifferent to the institutional church."[29]

Although America has plenty of Protestant evangelists seeking followers, Catholicism suffers a severe shortage of priests. Catholic News Service says 20,000 priests have quit since the 1950s (and one-fifth of priests violate their celibacy vows).[30] *National Catholic Reporter* says more than 10,000 devout American youths were in seminaries studying to be priests in 1965 - but the number of seminarians dropped to 3,400 by 2002.[31] *U.S. News & World Report* says the number of

American priests fell from 59,000 in 1975 to 41,500 in 2007 - even while the number of American Catholics boomed to 63 million.[32]

In 2009, Pew released an enlarged version of its Landscape survey saying multitudes "became unaffiliated because they do not believe in God or the teachings of most religions. Additionally, many people who left a religion to become unaffiliated say they did so in part because they think of religious people as hypocritical or judgmental, because religious organizations focus too much on rules, or because religious leaders are too focused on power and money."

The decline of American religiosity has far-reaching political implications, because the alliance of conservative believers with the Republican Party is undercut. Seculars, being more urban and cosmopolitan, generally vote Democratic. *Newsweek* noted: "Seventy-five percent of [religiously] unaffiliated voters chose Barack Obama."[33]

Another 2009 study by Harvard sociologist Robert Putnam, author of *Bowling Alone*, found that the share of "nones" among young Americans has risen to thirty to forty percent. "It's a huge change...a stunning development," Dr. Putnam said. "They grew up in a period in which being religious meant being politically conservative, especially on social issues," he noted, and they were repelled by "intolerance and rigidity and doctrinaire political views." He added: "That is the future of America. Their views and their habits religiously are going to persist and have a huge effect on the future."

Church scandals contribute to America's loss of faith. Child-molesting by Catholic priests tarnished the church's claim to moral superiority. Evangelist sex messes have done likewise. Cult suicides, jailing of Mormon polygamists, even murders in religious compounds - all these tainted the image of the pious.

As Harvard's Putnam observed, the Republican-evangelical alliance itself hastened the decline. ARIS director Silk commented:

"In the 1990s, it really sank in on the American public generally that there was a long-lasting 'religious right' connected to a political party, and that turned a lot of people the other way.... In an earlier time, people who would have been content to say, 'Well, I'm some kind of a Protestant,' now say, 'Hell no, I won't go.'"

EDUCATED CHURCHES DYING

Here's another indicator of slippage: America's mainline Protestant churches - elite, liberal, "tall steeple" denominations with seminary-trained ministers - decayed enormously in the past half-century. When I was young in the 1950s, these bodies were the pillars of respectability. Business leaders and professionals filled their pews. The "Seven Sisters of American Protestantism" - Presbyterians, Lutherans, Episcopalians, Methodists, American (northern) Baptists, Disciples of Christ and United Church of Christ - dominated the religious landscape and the country clubs. In social prestige, they towered above uncouth, less-educated evangelicals and fundamentalists.

But the Seven Sisters suffered drastic downsizing, losing nearly ten million members while America's population doubled. United Methodists shrank from 11 million members in

1960 to 7.9 million by 2008. The Presbyterian Church USA dropped from 4.1 million to 2.2 million. Episcopalians fell from 3.4 million to 2.1 million. Etc.[34]

In *The Empty Church: The Suicide of Liberal Christianity*, Thomas Reeves wrote: "As is quite well known, the mainline churches have been shrinking dramatically during the last three decades and appear to be confused and helpless." He added: "In 1995, a researcher observed that the Methodist Church had lost one thousand members every week for the last thirty years." Actually, Methodism's loss has been a bit worse. The church's three million drop from 1960 to 2008 averages twelve hundred per week.

The mainline misery didn't ease in the twenty-first century. The 2008 ARIS survey said the tall-steeple denominations, "whose proportion of the American population shrank from 18.7 percent in 1990 to 17.2 percent in 2001, all experienced sharp numerical declines this decade and now constitute just 12.9 percent." ARIS director Silk commented: "It looks like the two-party system of American Protestantism - mainline versus evangelical - is collapsing. A generic form of evangelicalism is emerging as the normative form of non-Catholic Christianity in the United States."

All this implies that educated Americans, the mainline constituency, no longer need supernatural faith. Church growth is among the less-educated. America's pattern is clear: highbrow religion is dying; lowbrow religion is thriving.

Meanwhile, citing research by the Fuller Institute and the George Barna religious polling service, Pastoral Care Inc. of Oklahoma wrote:

"Over 4,000 churches closed in America last year. Over 1,700 pastors left the ministry every month last year. Over 3,500 people a day left the church last year."

RELIGIOUS TABOOS GONE

Finally, here's more proof of America's religious decline: Church taboos that ruled society in the 1950s have vanished like the snows of yesteryear. In those days, it was a crime for stores to open on the sabbath - and you could be jailed for buying a cocktail or lottery ticket - or for looking at the equivalent of a Playboy magazine or a sexy R-rated movie. Even writing about sex was censored. It was a crime in some states to sell birth-control devices; elsewhere, buying a condom was hush-hush. It was a felony to be gay; homosexuals were imprisoned under biblical "sodomy" laws. (One I remember committed suicide, rather than face trial.) Unmarried couples could be collared by cops for sharing a bedroom. No proper hotelier would rent to a suspicious-looking pair. An unwed girl who became pregnant was disgraced, along with her family. Abortion was a prison offense, and desperate young women died of illicit termination attempts. Sex education was denounced from pulpits. Divorce was unmentionable.

Also at that time, Jews were excluded from "Christian-only" clubs, and women were excluded from most occupations. Blacks were consigned to segregation, like Indians on reservations. They weren't allowed into white schools, restaurants, hotels, theaters, pools or neighborhoods. Mixed-race marriage was a crime.

Of course, in the hodgepodge of life, there

21

were exceptions to all those 1950s strictures, and rebels against them. Bootleggers, hookers, bookies, free spirits and bawdy cynics existed. But law and officialdom were on the side of taboos.

Today, a half-century later, morality has flip-flopped. Unwed couples now live together openly with the blessing of their families. Children of single moms are welcomed like other kids. Blacks are guaranteed legal equality. Women's job rights are assured by law. Gay sex no longer is a crime. Gambling isn't merely legal - it's run by the state. Sexual movies and magazines are so common they're boring. Liquor clubs are everywhere. Sunday is a whopper shopper day.

How could morality change so much in a single lifetime? Why do most of us seniors hardly notice the amazing transformation that occurred? Sometimes, when I recall the societal proscriptions of our youth, they seem unreal, lost in the mist of the past.

Clearly, stigmas of puritanical religion lost their power in the second half of the twentieth century. American society progressed, leaving the bluenose mentality behind. Actually, today's tolerant values, accepting yesterday's outcasts, are more decent, fair and humane.

TO THE THIRD WORLD

Most observers think religion will remain powerful in America for generations to come. Although mainline Protestant churches are following Europe's disappearing act, and twenty million have drifted from Catholicism, the fundamentalist-evangelical-Pentecostal-Mormon conservative realm retains great strength. However, some researchers contend

22

that even this born-again community is weakening. *The Fall of the Evangelical Nation: The Surprising Crisis Inside the Church*, by journalist Christine Wicker, says the vaunted might of fundamentalists has been grossly exaggerated. She begins her book:

"Evangelical Christianity in America is dying. The great evangelical movements of today are not a vanguard. They are a remnant, unraveling at every edge. Look at it any way you like: Conversions. Baptisms. Membership. Retention. Participation. Giving. Attendance. Religious literacy. Effect on culture. All are down and dropping."

In a 2009 *Christian Science Monitor* essay titled "The Coming Evangelical Collapse," religion writer Michael Spencer pronounced the same verdict. He began:

"We are on the verge - within ten years - of a major collapse of evangelical Christianity. This breakdown will follow the deterioration of the mainline Protestant world and it will fundamentally alter the religious and cultural environment in the West. Within two generations, evangelicalism will be a house deserted of half its occupants."

It's too early to know whether these forecasts will prove correct. But it isn't too early to observe another visible trend: Religion is leaving the First World and shifting to the less-educated, low-income Third World.

Faith remains powerful in Islamic lands, where harsh religious laws mandate stoning women to death for adultery, chopping off hands and feet of transgressors, flogging of alcohol drinkers, execution of "blasphemers" - and where fervent belief spurs hundreds of young "martyrs" to volunteer as suicide bombers.

In southern tropics, in Africa, South Asia and Latin America, all forms of Christianity are booming, emotionally, primitively, even violently. The world's largest Methodist district now is the Ivory Coast. Hidebound Anglicans from Africa outnumber Englishmen at Lambeth World Conferences, scuttling attempts by English Anglicans to accommodate gays and women. Muslim-Christian riots flare repeatedly in Nigeria. Thousands of Santeria animal sacrifices occur in Mestizo Hispanic countries (and immigrants perform some in Miami, polluting waterways with animal bodies).

Pennsylvania State University scholar Philip Jenkins wrote *The Next Christendom* foreseeing an ugly future in which teeming, simplistic, Third World Christians become a militant danger similar to today's Muslim extremists. While Christianity fades in the First World, Dr. Jenkins says, it is surging in the underdeveloped tropics: "currently 480 million in Latin America, 360 million in Africa, and 313 million in Asia."

Third World Christians tend to be magic-oriented, seeing faith as a shield against demons, witches, evil dreams, bad luck, and such superstition. In a long excerpt reprinted in *The Atlantic*, Dr. Jenkins wrote:

"They interpret the horrors of everyday urban life in supernatural terms. In many cases, these churches seek to prove their spiritual powers in struggles against witchcraft. The intensity of belief in witchcraft across much of Africa can be startling. As recently as last year [2001] at least one thousand alleged witches were hacked to death in a single 'purge' in the

Democratic Republic of the Congo. Far from declining with urbanization, fear of witches has intensified. Since the collapse of South Africa's apartheid regime in 1994, witchcraft has emerged as a primary social fear in Soweto, with its three million impoverished residents."

(Remember the African evangelist who visited the Pentecostal church of Alaska Gov. Sarah Palin, laid hands on her head, and asked God to shield her from witches?)

Professor Jenkins says armed Christian militants such as "the terrifying Lord's Resistance Army in Uganda" commit slaughter. "The Holy Spirit Mobile Force, also pledged to fight witches.... engaged in a holy war against [the Ugandan government]. Holy Spirit soldiers, many of them children and young teenagers, were ritually anointed with butter on the understanding that is would make them bulletproof." It didn't work, and the Christian uprising was crushed.

"In 2000, more than a thousand people in another Ugandan sect, the Movement for the Restoration of the Ten Commandments of God, perished in an apparent mass suicide," he added.

These are extreme examples, but they show a gulf between First World and Third World Christianity - and warn of potential danger. Dr. Jenkins noted:

"Recent violence between Muslims and Christians raises the danger that Nigerian society might be brought to ruin by the clash of jihad and crusade. Muslims and Christians are at each other's throats in Indonesia, the Philippines, Sudan, and a growing number of other African nations; Hindu extremists persecute Christians in India. Demographic projections suggest that these feuds will simply worsen."

As religion recedes in the First World and blossoms in the Third World, it's arguable that the former is the winner and the latter the loser.

Slowly, quietly, imperceptibly, faith is fading in Western democracies. A long-term shift of civilization is occurring, but most of us are too busy to notice.

1. Will and Ariel Durant, *The Age of Voltaire*, 1965.

2. B.R. Redman, *The Portable Voltaire*, 1949.

3. Letter to John Adams, April 11, 1823.

4. Letter to Correa de Serra, April 11, 1820.

5. Letter to Dr. Benjamin Waterhouse, June 26, 1822.

6. London lectures, quoted by Rodney Stark in *Sociology of Religion*, Fall 1999.

7. Crawley, *The Tree of Life*, 1905, London: Hutchinson & Co.

8. Wallace, *Religion: An Anthropological View*, 1966.

9. *The New York Times*, April 25, 1968, "A Bleak Outlook is Seen for Religion."

10. NBC News, April 20, 2005. "Church Struggles with Attendance in Europe."

11. *Newsweek*, Aug. 15, 2005. "Near the Edge of the Abyss."

12. Ibid.

13. *The Washington Post*, April 17, 2005.

14. *Harvard Divinity Bulletin*, Jan. 1, 1994.

15. Who is Secular in the World Today? - international symposium of the Institute for the Study of Secularism in Society and Culture, reported in *Religion in the News*, Fall 2006.

16. *Boston Globe*, May 2, 2005, "Catholic Church Withers in Europe."

17. Steve Bruce, *God is Dead: Secularization in the West*, 2002, Blackwell Publishers.

18. Centre for Clergy Care book review, 2003.

19. Philip Jenkins, *The Next Christendom*, segment published in *The Atlantic*, October 2002.

20. *Spero News*, Dec. 6, 2005.

21. *Japan Times*, Jan. 1, 2002.

22. Who is Secular in the World Today? - a symposium by the Institute for the Study of Secularism in Society and Culture, reported as a supplement to *Religion in the News*, Fall 2006.

23. Ibid.

24. CNN News, April 30, 2009.

25. *Tampa Tribune*, Feb. 8, 2008.

26. Michael Shermer, *How We Believe: The Search for God in an Age of Science*.

27. Peter Berger, *The Desecularization of the World*, 1999, Eerdsmans Publishing Co.

28. *Newsweek*, April 13, 2009.

29. *National Catholic Reporter*, February, 2002.

30. Catholic News Service, Feb. 10, 2009.

31. *National Catholic Reporter*, February, 2002.

32. *U.S. News & World Report*, April 18, 2008.

33. *Newsweek*, April 13, 2009.

34. 2009 *Yearbook of American and Canadian Churches.*

(from *Free Inquiry* magazine - Feb-March 2010)

28

Chapter 2

EMPTY TEMPLES

Some American cities are suffering a new problem: abandoned churches. *The Philadelphia Inquirer* reported that officials in the City of Brotherly Love can't cope with once-stately temples that "decay into neighborhood eyesores."

"There are now so many shuttered houses of worship - at least 300 estimated across the Philadelphia region - that anxiety over what to do with them has spread beyond religious circles and into City Hall and suburban town councils," the newspaper said.

As young people drift away from religion, and aging members die off, vacant "tall steeple" edifices are like the bones of formerly mighty dinosaurs.

"In the Roman Catholic Archdiocese of Philadelphia, which has closed dozens of parishes in the past 20 years and nine this year, weekly Sunday Mass attendance is about 18 percent, a quarter of what it was two generations ago," the *Inquirer* reported.

A few months earlier, the *Detroit Free Press* reported that the Motor City is experiencing the same phenomenon. "Historic, skyline-defining landmarks, cavernous works of Old World artisanship," are sinking into oblivion, the paper said. One Michigan real estate dealer "has listings for more than 50 churches in metro Detroit alone."

Every American city presents an impressive array of sacred architecture - citadels where generations prayed to invisible spirits - but the relentless rise of the new Secular Age threatens to turn many of them into derelicts.

Evidence of religion's decline in America keeps snowballing, month after month. Some 2012 items:

-- A nationwide Gallup survey found that one-third of people no longer participate. "Another 32 percent of Americans are nonreligious, based on their statement that religion is not an important part of their daily life and that they seldom or never attend religious services," the poll summary said.

-- The ten-year U.S. Religious Census published by the Association of Religion Data Archives listed 158 million Americans - half the population - as "unclaimed" by any church.

-- A Pew Research Center poll found that 19 percent of Americans - nearly one-fifth of the population - select "none" as their religious preference.

What's the correct tally of the churchless - one-third, half or one-fifth? Although surveys strive for accuracy, they can't seem to reach precise agreement amid their varied approaches to questioning.

What's abundantly clear, however, is that the ratio of American "nones" has soared, dramatically and rapidly, since the 1990s. Church attendance is down; money donations are down; supernatural beliefs are down. Perhaps 50 million U.S. adults now ignore organized religion. All data indicate that America is following Western Europe into the scientific-minded Secular Era. It's another historic transition for civilization.

And lofty temples that once rang with piety are sinking into neglect.

(from *Free Inquiry* - Dec. 2012 / Jan. 2013)

Chapter 3

CLERGY WHO QUIT

Another indicator of religious decline in America is the significant number of clergy who cease believing the supernatural tenets of their churches.

Deep, deep inside, some preachers gradually sense that their lives are devoted to fantasy. They come to suspect that creeds, dogmas and scriptures about deities and devils, heavens and hells, miracles and messiahs, are fiction. But they don't dare reveal such qualms, lest they wreck their careers, their status, and their pensions. So they hedge in the pulpit, speaking in metaphors, living a pose.

However, a few have integrity enough to chuck it all - to throw away everything they worked hard to attain, and publicly disavow their past beliefs. Such traumatic reversals require courage and honesty.

A couple of my friends, Richard and Dotty Kendig, grew up in fundamentalist families, were married in Bible college, were ordained, and became missionaries to Peru. They were deeply compassionate and truly desired to help primitive Amazon villagers. But they were repelled as they watched fellow missionaries abuse the natives, treat them with contempt, and count them only as "souls" to be added to the convert list. Some missionaries forced native women to cover their bodies, and stormed into huts to smash yucca beer pots. After 15 years, the Kendigs quit, leaving with humanist values.

"We went there to convert the Indians, and they converted us," Dick sometimes told me. He and Dotty subsequently tried preaching in Pennsylvania churches, but felt awash in hypocrisy. They quit Christianity, became freethinking Unitarians, and moved to a remote West Virginia farm, where Dick was killed by an overturning tractor. His widow is now a schoolteacher.

How many other ministers undergo this type of pilgrim's progress, slowly abandoning supernatural faith? Here are some famous cases:

CHARLES TEMPLETON

Growing up in Toronto, Templeton was afire with intelligence and creativity. He became a teen-age sports cartoonist for the *Globe and Mail* newspaper. Later he experienced an emotional conversion, started his own church, and rose rapidly to be Canada's top evangelist in the 1940s. He became a major broadcast preacher. He teamed up with Billy Graham for huge revivals in arenas across America and Europe, "saving" thousands. Together, they spread Youth For Christ International.

But Templeton began having intellectual problems with fundamentalism. Trying to make his religion rational, he earned a degree from Princeton Theological Seminary, then became a special preacher for the National Council of Churches, then became head of evangelism for the Presbyterian Church USA.

The changes didn't save his church career. His doubts wiped out his faith. In 1957, he announced that he was an agnostic and renounced Christianity - stunning the evangelical world in which he had been a superstar.

Templeton's drive swiftly took him to new achievements. He became a Canadian television commentator - then managing editor of the *Toronto Star* - then a leader of the Ontario Liberal Party - then an advertising executive - then editor of *Maclean's* Magazine - then host of a long-running daily radio show. By the 1980s, he had retired mostly into writing, turning out novels and nonfiction books.

In the 1990s, just before Alzheimer's beset him, Templeton summed up his religious transformation in *Farewell to God: My Reasons for Rejecting the Christian Faith*. It was another slam to the church community that once adored him.

His book says Christianity rests on "fables" that no scientific-thinking person can swallow. The church teaches "beliefs that are outdated, demonstrably untrue, and often, in their various manifestations, deleterious to individuals and to society," the former evangelist wrote.

Page after page, he lists Bible miracles that are absurd to modern minds. Then he asks how an all-merciful father-creator could have made such a cruel universe:

"All life is predicated on death. Every

carnivorous creature must kill and devour another creature. It has no option.... Why does God's grand design require creatures with teeth designed to crush spines or rend flesh, claws fashioned to seize and tear, venom to paralyze, mouths to suck blood, coils to constrict and smother - even expandable jaws so that prey may be swallowed whole and alive?... Nature is, in Tennyson's vivid phrase, 'red in tooth and claw,' and life is a carnival of blood.... How could a loving and omnipotent God create such horrors?"

His book concludes: "I believe that there is no supreme being with human attributes - no God in the biblical sense - but that all life is the result of timeless evolutionary forces.... I believe that, in common with all living creatures, we die and cease to exist."

Templeton died and ceased to exist in 2001.

MARJOE GORTNER

Instead of writing a book about his apostasy, Gortner made a movie.

He was a remarkable denizen of the underbelly of religion. His parents were California evangelists leading revivals that were money-making hokum. Onstage, they exchanged secret signals while manipulating worshippers to emotional peaks and extracting large offerings from them. They sold "holy" gimmicks guaranteed to heal the sick.

They named their son Marjoe for Mary and Joseph, and trained him as a squeaky child preacher, a religious sensation. They drilled him in sermons and stage antics, sometimes holding his head underwater to force him to memorize his lines, Marjoe later recounted.

At age three, he was ordained by the Church of the Old-Time Faith. At four, he performed a wedding, triggering an uproar that caused California legislators to forbid marriages by preachers under 21.

For ten years, Marjoe the boy wonder performed across the South and Midwest Bible Belt. He estimated that his parents raked in $3 million. Then Marjoe ran off at 14 and lived with an older woman who served as both lover and surrogate mother. Eventually he returned to the revival circuit, strutting and prancing onstage as his parents had taught him. Money rolled in again.

Gortner knew that his religious act was a sham. Yet, strangely, he had an honest streak and decided to expose his own fraud. He engaged a film crew to make a documentary about his ministry. After revival shows, the cameras followed the preacher to hotel rooms where he tossed armfuls of money, crowing, "Thank you, Jesus!"

The film, *Marjoe*, jolted the fundamentalist world when it was released in 1972. As an ex-preacher, Gortner became a minor movie star and recording artist. He went bankrupt while attempting to produce a movie about a crooked evangelist. In 1995, he appropriately played a preacher in Wild Bill.

During Gortner's heyday on the revival stage, another star was faith-healer A.A. Allen, who toured with jars containing bodies he said were demons he had cast out of the sick. (Doubters said they were frogs.) Allen disappeared after a show at Wheeling, West Virginia - and was found dead of alcoholism in a San Francisco hotel room, his pockets crammed with wads of cash.

Gortner said Allen once taught him how to tell when a revival is finished and it's time to travel to the next city: "When you can turn people on their head and shake them and no money falls out, you know God's saying, 'Move on, son.'"

JAMES BALDWIN

Some bookish Americans may not know that Baldwin, the great black author, formerly was a boy evangelist like Gortner.

Baldwin grew up in Harlem, where his tyrannical stepfather was pastor of Fireside Pentecostal Assembly. In a *New Yorker* essay titled "Down at the Cross," later published in his civil rights book, *The Fire Next Time*, Baldwin recounted the bitter hopelessness of the ghetto, where jobless men fought and drank themselves into the gutter.

The surrounding misery "helped to hurl me into the church," he wrote. As a child, at a prayer meeting, "everything came roaring, screaming, crying out, and I fell to the ground before the altar. It was the strangest sensation I have ever had in my life." Newly "saved," he became a 14-year-old junior preacher at the family church and soon was "a much bigger drawing card than my father."

"That was the most frightening time of my life, and quite the most dishonest, and the resulting hysteria lent great passion to my sermons - for a while," Baldwin wrote. Since crime and vice filled surrounding streets, he said, "it was my good luck - perhaps - that I found myself in the church racket instead of some other, and surrendered to a spiritual seduction long before I came to any carnal knowledge."

While he tingled to the "fire and excitement" of Pentecostalism, he nonetheless experienced "the slow crumbling of my faith." It occurred "when I began to read again.... I began, fatally, with Dostoevsky." He continued handing out gospel tracts, but knew privately that they were "impossible to believe."

"I was forced, reluctantly, to realize that the Bible itself had been written by men." He dismissed the claim that the Bible writers were divinely inspired, saying he "knew by now, alas, far more about divine inspiration than I dared admit, for I knew how I worked myself up into my own visions."

The ex-minister wrote that he might have stayed in the church if "there was any loving-kindness to be found" in it - but "there was no love in the church. It was a mask for hatred and self-hatred and despair."

At 17, Baldwin left religion behind forever. He later called himself a "nothing" theologically. Eventually, his switch to writing enriched the world of literature immensely. In "Down at the Cross," he summed up:

"Life is tragic simply because the Earth turns and the sun inexorably rises and sets, and one day, for each of us, the sun will go down for the last, last time. Perhaps the whole root of our trouble, the human trouble, is that we will sacrifice all the beauty of our lives, will imprison ourselves in totems, taboos, crosses, blood sacrifices, steeples, mosques, races, armies, flags, nations, in order to deny the fact of death, which is the only fact we have."

For Baldwin, the sun went down a last, last time in 1987.

DAN BARKER

How do supernatural beliefs die? Very slowly, year after year, in a thousand small expansions of the mind - according to Barker, who evolved from teen-age evangelist to co-president of the Freedom From Religion Foundation.

"It was a gradual process, a growth," he told an Iowa newspaper. "It would be like asking you, 'When did you grow up?' You probably could not answer that question with one defining moment."

At fifteen, Barker experienced a typical hysterical conversion at a California revival, then flung himself fervently into adolescent religiosity. He carried a Bible daily, joined fundamentalist youth groups, and preached to everyone in sight.

Keenly intelligent and a gifted musician, he rose rapidly in the teeming evangelical culture. His preaching and music-arranging blossomed for several years. He pastored small churches, married a gospel singer and they toured the revival circuit for eight years, rising toward success.

But doubts insidiously crept into Barker's innermost thoughts. Later, in his book, *Losing Faith in Faith: From Preacher to Atheist*, he explained:

"It was some time in 1979, turning thirty, when I started to have some early questions about Christianity.... I just got to the point where my mind was restless to move beyond the simplicities of fundamentalism.... So, not with any real purpose in mind, I began to satisfy this irksome intellectual hunger. I began to read some science magazines, some philosophy, psychology, daily newspapers (!), and began to

39

catch up on the liberal arts education I should have had years before. This triggered a ravenous appetite to learn, and produced a slow but steady migration across the theological spectrum that took about four or five years. I had no sudden, eye-opening experience. When you are raised as I was, you don't just snap your fingers and say, 'Oh, silly me! There's no God.'"

Painfully, during his backslide, he suffered shame as he continued leading church services. "I felt hypocritical, often hearing myself mouth words about which I was no longer sure, but words that the audience wanted to hear.... I became more and more embarrassed at what I used to believe, and more attracted to rational thinkers.... I no longer believed what I was preaching."

Barker frantically sought an escape from his dilemma. He began a side job in computer programming. His transformation wrecked his marriage. Finally, scrupulously conscientious, he wrote a mass letter to former church and gospel music colleagues, telling them: "I can no longer honestly call myself a Christian. You can probably imagine that it has been an agonizing process for me."

Today, Barker is married to Annie Laurie Gaylor, co-president of the Freedom From Religion Foundation - and is just as exuberant for intellectual honesty as he once was for fundamentalism.

JOHN W. LOFTUS

Evangelical congregations can be petty, vindictive, unforgiving - and this lack of compassion can help propel a minister into doubts and loss of faith. That's what happened to Loftus, formerly an intense Church of Christ pastor.

Why I Became an Atheist, an earnest autobiography, recounts how Loftus grew up in a Catholic home in Fort Wayne, Indiana, attending parochial school, without much religious commitment. In adolescence, he was a problem teen, kicked out of high school, sent to a juvenile home for repeated minor police troubles. Then he underwent an emotional conversion and became "on fire for God. I burned with passion for the Lord. And for good reason: I believed God turned my life around."

Loftus entered the rebellious "Jesus Freak" subculture and "witnessed" on street corners. Then he attended a Church of Christ seminary and became a pastor. But several congregational conflicts soured him on church life. A church board fired him because some leading parishioners thought (mistakenly) that his removal would win back a prominent couple who had moved to a different church. Then Loftus became active in another church, of which his cousin was pastor - but the cousin angrily suspected that Loftus was trying to grab his pulpit. Worst of all, a homeless shelter director, a former stripper, falsely accused Loftus of rape, and fellow Church of Christ leaders wouldn't defend him.

These and other squabbles caused the young minister to think deeply about religion - and the more he thought, the more it seemed a fantasy. He finally shifted to complete atheism, and found it liberating. While he was an evangelical, he suffered constant guilt and shame for his human frailties. But now he has no need to apologize. "Today, I am guilt-free."

ROBERT M. PRICE

A supreme nonconformist, Price went from born-again evangelist to atheist. He holds two doctorates and has written 40 books. He now contends that Jesus never existed as the Bible depicts him, but was a fabrication from many risen-savior magical legends of the Middle East. Yet Price attends a Christian church and calls himself a "Christian atheist." What a tangle!

Raised in a fundamentalist Baptist church, he led an Inter-Varsity Christian Fellowship in college and attended an evangelical seminary, where Billy Graham was his commencement speaker. Then he became pastor of a New Jersey Baptist church.

But he was ravenous to read and learn. Over two decades, he earned two theological doctorates from Drew University. His intense study wiped out his supernatural faith, and he left the pulpit in 1994. He dabbled with ultra-liberal Unitarian Universalism, but became disenchanted with that, as well.

He joined the Jesus Seminar, which tries to separate fables from historically accurate verses in the Bible. And he became a prolific author, pouring out volumes such as *Jesus is Dead, The Incredible Shrinking Son of Man, Deconstructing Jesus, The Reason-Driven Life*, etc.

His biography says he now "attends the Episcopal Church and keeps his mouth shut."

Other backsliding clergy handle their loss of faith in diverse ways. The legendary Mother Teresa was plagued for decades by secret inner doubts that either God or Jesus is real, and she

42

often confided that she was unable to pray - yet she lavished adoration on the deities in public appearances, and prayed before television cameras.

In contrast, the great mentor Will Durant almost was ordained a Catholic priest, but he ceased supernatural beliefs and withdrew from orders. Later, he gave a talk about phallus-worship in religion - and his bishop excommunicated him swiftly, announcing the action to newspapers. Durant's devout mother collapsed in shock and his father ordered him to leave their home.

Even seminary professors can slip from certainty. In *Walking Away From Faith*, Dr. Ruth A. Tucker of Calvin Theological Seminary in Grand Rapids, Michigan, wrote: "There are moments when I doubt all. It is then that I sometimes ask myself as I'm looking out my office window, 'What on earth am I doing here? They'd fire me if they only knew.'" She left the seminary in a bitter conflict, but remained religious, despite her doubts.

Similarly, Dr. Bart Ehrman, chairman of religious studies at the University of North Carolina, Chapel Hill, described in *Misquoting Jesus* how he journeyed from born-again Christian to agnostic.

In addition to clergy, multitudes of lay churchmen likewise cease believing. One was university librarian Edward Babinski, who told his own story and related several others in *Leaving the Fold*. Similarly, former *Los Angeles Times* religion reporter William Lobdell wrote *Losing My Religion: How I Lost My Faith Reporting on Religion in America*. Once a born-again evangelical, he slowly realized that intelligent people cannot swallow magical tales.

The process of secularization - erosion of supernatural beliefs in Western society - encompasses many who once were devout, but came to see church claims as fairy tales. In addition to the few ministers who make dramatic public breaks, how many more remain in the pulpit, reciting dogmas and creeds they no longer believe, afraid to face their real selves? Perhaps, like Tolstoy's Ivan Ilytch, in the final hour before death, they will see that their lives were meaningless.

(from *American Atheist*, August 2009)

Chapter 4

MORE OUT OF THE CLOSET

In recent years, a growing spotlight has illuminated clergy who admit they no longer believe supernatural church claims. Many suffer painful struggles and quit the pulpit. Others continue preaching, but use vague language to hide their hypocrisy and trick parishioners into thinking they're still devout.

Renowned biologist and atheist Richard Dawkins launched The Clergy Project, an online community where backsliding ministers - some anonymously - share their doubts and torments. From it, researchers Daniel Dennett and Linda LaScola published *Caught in the Pulpit: Leaving Belief Behind*, outlining "the disconnect between what closeted non-believing clergy believe and what they preach." Meanwhile, one veteran of The Clergy Project, former 25-year Louisiana Pentecostal preacher Jerry DeWitt, became leader of a group called Recovering from Religion. He told his story in a book, *Hope After Faith: An Ex-Pastor's Journey*

A *New York Times* report described how the soft-spoken ex-evangelist broke into sobs after he realized he no longer could pray with troubled parishioners. When his disbelief became known, he was fired from his city job, his wife left him, his home was foreclosed, and most of his family stopped speaking to him.

The Clergy Project has grown to more than 600 participants. The Stiefel Freethought Foundation donated $100,000 for "employment transition" aid to help ministers enter new careers. Here are a few testimonials:

Former Canadian Anglican priest Jeffrey Olsson:

"I still remember one pivotal morning. I lay in bed, the warm summer sun streaming into my window. It dawned on me for the first time after 32 years of committed Christian life that the world makes much more sense without a God in it. All the violence, all the chaos, pain and suffering. Where is our loving God?... Deep inside, I secretly knew I was no longer fit for ministry."

The Rev. John Compere:

"I was a fifth-generation Baptist minister, ordained at 18, while in college. I served until age 32 when I left the ministry and the church.... Leaving the ministry was not an easy decision to make... but it was a decision I ultimately HAD to make if I didn't want to risk being publicly phony and privately cynical. I became an agnostic, then an atheist, NOT because I hadn't read the Bible, but because I had! An atheist, by the way, is simply someone who does not believe in a supernatural being. I am convinced that the evidence supports that view."

The Rev. Mike Aus said that, after leaving a Lutheran church in Texas and quitting the ministry, he was "not falling from faith," but instead was "rising to reason."

Former Church of Ireland rector Patrick Semple said he finally confessed to his bishop that he had become an atheist - but the bishop simply shrugged and told him to "get back to work." When he told a fellow cleric about it, the comrade replied: "Join the gang."

Former Catholic priest Tom Rastrelli said he was sickened by child molestation by fellow priests. "As the abuse scandal worsened and more bishops denied the crimes they'd committed, my belief in church as a divine institution faded.... No longer believing in the inspiration of the scriptures, I became a fully fledged agnostic. Within another few months, I was comfortable saying that I didn't believe in a god. I was no longer afraid of what people thought of me, of the negative stigma surrounding the word 'atheist.' I felt free to be a fully realized human being. Thousands of years of canonized fear, loathing, shame and distrust vanished. I owned being an atheist."

American Presbyterian minister John Shuck is an odd exception. He publicly declares that he doesn't believe in God, Jesus, heaven, hell, miracles or other supernatural teachings - yet he remains a pastor accepted by his flock and fellow clergy. As for other ministers, he says, "many appreciate what I am doing, as they have many of the same convictions."

Varying personal accounts of fading faith were voiced by Joe Armstrong, Catherine Dunphy, Paul Gallagher, Teresa MacBain, Kevin

Hegarty and other clergy.

It's another facet of the slippage of religion in Western democracies.

Chapter 5

CREEPING SECULAR HUMANISM

Few people notice, but a profound shift is discernible in history and current trends: Values of secular humanism - improving people's lives, without supernaturalism - are gaining ground, decade after decade, century after century. They're becoming the standard of civilization, overcoming past ugliness.

Evidence confirms that wars are diminishing, democracy is spreading, dictatorships are fading, health is brightening, human rights are growing, personal brutality is lessening, illiteracy is retreating, longevity is increasing, etc.

These hopeful changes may be overlooked amid torments in the daily news, of which there are plenty: Suicide terror attacks massacre defenseless people. Tornados, tsunamis, earthquakes and floods inflict tragedy. Perhaps 20 million Americans are jobless, and fallout from the Great Recession hurts the world. Overpopulation causes pollution and global

49

warming. Millions of young women are subjugated in less-developed nations or forced into prostitution. Inequality between rich and poor keep worsening.

Nonetheless, human life is getting better. First, consider the ultimate madness, war:

Bloodshed from conflicts has decreased amazingly over the centuries, according to three new books by major university scholars. Harvard psychologist Steven Pinker says war deaths as a percentage of population are only one-thousandth as bad today as in gory past epochs.

"It is easy to forget how dangerous life used to be, how deeply brutality was once woven into the fabric of daily existence," Dr. Pinker wrote in *The Better Angels of Our Nature: Why Violence Has Declined*.

He begins his 700-page book by recounting horrors once commonplace, such as massacres, rapes, sacrifices and slavery in the Bible. The Old Testament outlines 1.2 million violent deaths, he estimates. By the Middle Ages, torture and cruelty were rampant in the Inquisition and in punishments by kings. Reviewing Pinker's book, Cambridge scholar David Runciman wrote:

"It is hard not to be occasionally struck dumb by just how horrible people used to be. The image I can't get out of my head is of a hollow brass cow used for roasting people alive. Its mouth was left open so that their screams would sound like the cow was mooing, adding to the amusement of onlookers."

Dr. Pinker calculates that the ratio of people killed by warfare was 500 per 100,000 in ancient times - which dropped to 60 per 100,000 during the violent 20th century - and now it's a mere three-tenths of a person per 100,000. That's more than a thousandfold decrease in war deaths per-capita.

His war finding is corroborated by two other new books: *Winning the War on War*, by American University professor Joshua Goldstein. and *Human Security Report 2009-2010*, by Andrew Mack of Simon Fraser University in Canada. Dr. Goldstein's book declares:

"Despite all the hand-wringing, fearmongering and bad-news headlines, peace is on the rise. Fewer wars are starting, more are ending, and those that remain are smaller and more localized than in past years. Incredibly, no national armies are still fighting one another; all of today's wars are civil wars.... Today's successes in building peace have grown out of decades of effort and sacrifice by people working through international organizations, humanitarian aid agencies and popular movements around the world. At the center of this drama is the United Nations and its 60-year experiment in peacekeeping - overwhelmingly supported by American public opinion."

Dr. Mack says cultures have changed so that war no longer seems heroic or a source of national pride. "Wars of colonial conquest would be unthinkable today," he wrote, adding:

"Two seismic political shifts, the demise of colonialism and the end of the Cold War, removed major sources of tension and conflict from the international system. The percentage of countries with democratic governments doubled between 1950 and 2008, from 29 percent to 58 percent. Since democracies almost never go to war against each other, there have been progressively fewer countries around the world likely to fight each other.... High-intensity wars, those that kill at least 1,000 people a year, have declined by 78 percent since 1988."

In *Better Angels*, Dr. Pinker goes beyond warfare to outline other trends away from brutality and bigotry, toward tolerance and nurture - the goals of secular humanism. He says:

-- Murder in Europe has declined from nearly 100 people per 100,000 in medieval times to about one per 100,000 now.

-- Rape in the United States has fallen 80 percent since 1973. Lynchings, which once averaged 150 per year, have ceased.

-- The world had fewer than 20 democracies in 1946. Now there are almost 100. The number of totalitarian regimes has dropped from almost 90 in 1976 to about 25 now.

Pinker says the overall transition to a more humane world is "maybe the most important thing that has ever happened in human history."

The almost-disappearance of slavery is a shining example. The end of South Africa's apartheid is another.

Meanwhile, a new report, *2011 State of the Future*, was released by the Millennium Project, a worldwide study group created by the United Nations, the Smithsonian Institution and others. Looking back over the past quarter-century, it spells out that average life expectancy around the planet climbed from 64 years in the mid-1980s to 68 today - and that infant mortality worldwide fell from 70 deaths per 100,000 population to 40 today, dropping almost by half - and the ratio of people living on less than $1.25 per day declined from 43 percent of humanity to just 23 percent now, another drop of nearly half - and the number of wars dropped from 37 in the mid-1980s to 26 today.

Plenty of ugly problems remain. The Millennium report summarizes:

"The world is getting richer, healthier, better educated, more peaceful and better connected, and people are living longer, yet half the world is potentially unstable. Food prices are rising, water tables are falling, corruption and organized crime are increasing, environmental viability for our life support is diminishing, debt and economic insecurity are increasing, climate change continues, and the gap between the rich and poor continues to widen dangerously."

The report adds that "90 percent of 950 natural disasters in 2010 were weather-related and fit climate change models. These disasters killed 295,000 people and cost approximately $130 billion." Environmentalist Bill McKibben forecasts worse tragedy as global warming escalates.

Bottom line: Despite a multitude of afflictions, human life keeps improving. Gradually, humane values - rights spurred by the Enlightenment - are fixed ever-tighter into civilization. (Is it mere coincidence that religion is fading dramatically in the West as human betterment increases?)

Reducing violence and improving human rights requires many struggles - mostly led by liberal reformers who defeat conservative resistance. Look back over the past century in America and a pattern is obvious:

Women gained the right to vote, couples won the right to practice birth control, Social Security and other New Deal "safety net" reforms bolstered families, black Americans gradually attained legal equality, Medicare and Medicaid brought health security to millions, and a stride toward universal health insurance for all Americans occurred in 2010.

Humanism means striving to make things better for humanity. Secular means functioning without religion. Secular humanists throughout history generally have been crusaders for human rights, democracy, peace, health, education, nutrition, equality and other life-sustaining goals.

Values of secular humanism, from curbing war to improving everyday life, slowly are dominating most of the world. Whether there's a connection or not, the improvement coincides with the gradual retreat of religion.

(adapted from *Free Inquiry* - Feb-March, 2012)

Chapter 6

POLITICAL IMPLICATIONS

White evangelicals and fundamentalists are the heart of America's Republican Party. They comprise the renowned "religious right." Meanwhile, "nones", who don't attend church generally have liberal social beliefs and vote Democratic. In recent presidential elections, roughly three-fourths of white evangelicals voted Republican, while three-fourths of "nones" chose the opposite party.

Obviously, growing secularism has political implications that may shift the nation toward more progressive values. With churches fading and secularism climbing, a Democratic tide is rising. Sociologist Ruy Teixeira wrote in 2013 about America's religious demographics:

"In 1944, eighty percent of adults were white Christians. But things have changed a lot since then. Today, only about 52 percent of adults are white Christians. By 2024, that figure will be down to 45 percent. That means that, by the election of 2016, the United States will have ceased to be a white Christian nation. Looking even farther down the road, by 2040 white Christians will be only around 35 percent of the population, and conservative white Christians, who have been such a critical part of the Republican base, only about a third of that - a minority within a minority."

Part of the transformation stems from straight demographics, because minorities - Hispanics, Asians, blacks, Pacific Islanders, native Americans and the like - are growing strongly while traditional European whites barely hold steady. Before 2040, the Census Bureau projects, such whites will slip below half of the population.

In addition, Dr. Teixeira says loss of church membership is a boon to Democrats. "Between 2007 and 2012," he wrote, "...those who are religiously unaffiliated have gone from 15 to nearly 20 percent of adults. This is an astonishing rate of change."

After the 2012 election, *Washington Post* columnist Michael Gerson wrote that "nones" have become the largest single bloc of Democratic Party supporters, at 24 percent - while "religious conservatives remain the largest constituency within the Republican Party. So America is moving in the direction of having one secular party and one religious party, bringing polarization to a new level of intensity."

A few years ago, just after Republican George W. Bush won a second term, I wrote the following:

Bizarrely, the 2004 U.S. presidential election was decided by voters who oppose the theory

56

of evolution, or await the Rapture, or speak in the "unknown tongue," or seek faith-healing, or send money to television preachers, or think Satan is a real spirit stalking America.

White evangelicals and fundamentalists - mostly puritanical people who hate homosexuality, abortion, stem cell research, Hollywood, etc., and who tend to favor guns and the death penalty - tipped the ballot balance to their hero, President Bush. The "three G's" - God, guns and gays - were a crucial factor in the squeaker election. Exit polls credited born-again voters who ranked "moral values" as their chief concern, more important than the Iraq war, job losses and other issues.

"There are roughly 70 million people in America who do not believe in evolution, and those are Bush supporters," Pulitzer Prize-winning journalist Seymour Hersh said just before the election. Other estimates of what one cynic called the "Bigoted Christian Redneck" realm range as high as 100 million, counting narrow-minded members of mainline churches. This segment of the U.S. population isn't monolithic, either denominationally or politically. Nonetheless, it's a mighty force in the electorate.

How did the Religious Right rise to power? It's a long story, involving America's amazing moral change over the past half-century. Ponder this social history:

In the 1960s, the historic civil rights movement and the youth rebellion brought America's liberal heyday. Young protesters fought the Vietnam draft, blacks marched for equality, courts struck down censorship, and human rights laws were passed. The sexual revolution snowballed. Bigotry became unlawful. Despite the adolescent excesses of the 1960s, it was a time of moral improvement, in my view. Many old prejudices and taboos were swept aside.

Then a backlash occurred in the 1970s and '80s. Fundamentalists, who previously had seemed a mere fringe, began mobilizing against the wave of "wickedness" that had arrived. Historic U.S. Supreme Court rulings in 1962 and '63 against government-led school prayer, plus the 1973 opinion legalizing women's right to choose abortion, along with the easing of social stigmas against gays, etc., all convinced them that Satan was gaining control of America.

Evangelist Jerry Falwell coalesced this group by forming the Moral Majority. He demanded restoration of school prayer, crackdowns on porn, recriminalization of abortion, ostracism of gays, etc. This group yearned for a return to the "moral" 1950s - seemingly unaware that it had been a time of harsh prejudice. It was more proof of the age-old axiom that the most intolerant people in any society are religious hard-liners.

Although fundamentalists are mostly blue-collar folks, and previously had tended to be Democrats, they began finding a home in the Republican Party. In 1980, they were instrumental in electing Ronald Reagan president. When the Moral Majority faded, it was replaced by evangelist Pat Robertson's Christian Coalition, again solidly Republican. Robertson himself sought the GOP nomination for president.

Gradually, white evangelicals and fundamentalists became a wing of the GOP - anchoring the "base" that strategist Karl Rove milks for votes. The group is especially devoted to George W. Bush because he underwent an emotional conversion after years of heavy drinking - which makes him their hero, "one of us." Conservative Catholics joined this base.

Meanwhile, liberal mainline Protestant churches - which advocate somewhat more tolerant and humane values - have shrunk in America, losing millions of members. The national tide has flowed toward fundamentalism and narrow morality.

Today, some in the latter camp even say born-again President Jimmy Carter isn't a real Christian because he doesn't embrace the Religious Right political agenda. He quit the Southern Baptist Church in protest of its hidebound outlook. Oddly, Carter's piety would have galled many U.S. voters around 1970, but by 1976 the evangelical upsurge buoyed him, yet now he's reviled by the same group. A cycle has been completed.

So, today, born-again whites are a potent political element in the United States. Over the past decade, many researchers have found that Americans who attend church more than once a week are the most ardent Republican voters - while those who don't worship generally vote Democratic. This gives the GOP a huge power base, because America is more religious than other advanced nations.

Is this lineup permanent? I hope not. Although the future is unforeseeable, thinking people should hope that America gradually will follow Europe, Australia and other societies where churchgoing has faded. U.S. secularism is rising. In 1993, the National Opinion Research Center at the University of Chicago found that only 9 percent of U.S. respondents said they have no religion, but this group rose to 14 percent by 2002. During the same period, the ratio of Americans identifying themselves as Protestants fell from 63 to 52 percent.

Two 2004 reports - by the Pew Forum on Religion and Public Life and the Institute for Jewish and Community Research - both raised the "none" group to 16 percent of the U.S. population. This trend toward rationality, away from supernaturalism, someday may weaken the Religious Right.

Right now, however, America must endure a political powerhouse of mean-spirited believers who can sway elections. For the good of the nation, let's hope that 2004 was the nadir, and an upward path lies ahead.

(from *Free Inquiry* - February-March 2005)

Chapter 7

SECULAR SURGE

Gods, devils, heavens, hells, angels, demons, miracles, saviors, omens, prophecies, visions, ghosts, fairies, werewolves, imps, vampires, leprechauns, hexes, horoscopes, curses, charms, spells, etc., etc. Supernaturalism dominated humanity through uncountable centuries. Belief in spirits spawned human sacrifice, witch-hunts, holy wars, inquisitions and an astounding array of irrationality. The great poet William Butler Yeats wrote:

"Once every people in the world believed that trees were divine, and could take a human or grotesque shape and dance among the shadows; and that deer, and ravens and foxes, and wolves and bears, and clouds and pools, almost all things under the sun and moon, and the sun and moon, were not less divine and changeable. They saw in the rainbow the still-bent bow of a god thrown down in his negligence; they heard in the thunder the sound of his beaten water-jar, or the tumult of his chariot wheels; and when a sudden flight of wild ducks, or of crows, passed over their heads, they thought they were gazing at the dead hastening to their rest."[1]

The human mind, with its fearful imagination, concocted thousands of gods and spirits and magical marvels. But the human mind also possesses intelligent logic, which questioned supernatural claims. Slowly, thinking Westerners came to doubt that wraiths prowl the night and witches copulate with Satan. The Dark Ages and the Age of Faith yielded to the Renaissance, the Age of Reason and the Enlightenment. The scientific mentality - a desire for evidence - routed superstition.

Today, centuries of modern progress have erased a vast spectrum of invisible beings and magic. Only a handful of vague gods remain - and their substance constantly evaporates, like the Cheshire Cat, which faded to a vanishing smile. Western democracies are shifting to a new phase of civilization, the Secular Age. Religion is leaving the advanced, educated First World. It is retreating to the poor, backward Third World and, of course, Islamic lands.

America is experiencing an "atheism awakening," *The New York Times* says.[2] Open denial of supernatural religion has flared as a remarkable cultural phenomenon of the new twenty-first century. Past taboos that forced skeptics to stay silent, or consigned them to a little-known "freethought" fringe, are being obliterated.

To the surprise of the publishing industry, big sales were achieved by a wave of religion-bashing books: *The End of Faith* by Sam Harris, W.W. Norton, 2004 - *The God Delusion* by Richard Dawkins, Houghton Mifflin, 2006 - *Breaking the Spell* by Daniel Dennett, Viking, 2006 - *Letter to a Christian Nation* by Harris, Alfred A. Knopf, 2006 - *God is Not Great* by

Christopher Hitchens, Hachette Book Group, 2007. More are in the works.

Old-line agnostic organizations such as the Council for Secular Humanism, American Atheists, the Freedom from Religion Foundation and the Society for Ethical Culture have been joined by a flood of new groups: the Coalition of Reason, The Brights, the Secular Coalition for America, the Student Secular Alliance, and the like. Skeptic student clubs have sprouted on 174 American college and university campuses. Three universities have hired "humanist chaplains" to counsel nonreligious students, and other schools are under pressure to do likewise.

Doubters are taking conspicuous actions. New York's Coalition of Reason posted subway ads saying: "A million New Yorkers are good without God. Are You?" Other branches in Texas, Arizona, Idaho and West Virginia placed billboards proclaiming: "Don't Believe in God? You Are Not Alone." Indiana atheists published ads affirming: "You can be good without God." This 2009 American wave followed a larger British project in which signs on eight hundred buses declared: "There's probably no God. Now stop worrying and enjoy your life."

Good Without God: What a Billion Nonreligious People Do Believe, by Harvard's humanist chaplain, Greg Epstein, was released in 2009. Publisher William Morrow says the book "highlights humanity's potential for goodness and ways in which Humanists lead lives of purpose and compassion.... In short, Humanism teaches us that we can lead good and moral lives without supernaturalism, without higher powers - without God."

Psychological self-help groups for

Americans "recovering from religion" are sprouting. Dr. Darrel Ray in Kansas City and psychologist Linda Ford Blaikie in New York are among counselors offering group therapy to people who spent years praying to gods, then felt shaken after concluding that the divine spirits are imaginary. Blaikie was raised a devout Catholic but lost supernatural beliefs in college. "What happened in the next three years felt like a divorce," she says. Quitters like her suffer withdrawal pangs. "They lost their comfort, their Daddy, their community, their rosary beads, their protection," Blaikie said.

Multitudes of news reports have analyzed the dramatic rise of "nones" in surveys asking Americans their faith. Like many other outlets, CNN reported that "no religion" is "the fastest-growing religious identification in the United States."[3] opinion on

Oxford University Press's great reference compendium, *World Christian Encyclopedia*, written by devout churchgoers, lamented:

"No one in 1900 expected the massive defections from Christianity that subsequently took place in Western Europe due to secularism, in Russia and later Eastern Europe due to communism, and in the Americas due to materialism.... The number of nonreligionists... throughout the 20th century has skyrocketed from 3.2 million in 1900 to 697 million in 1970 and on to 918 million in AD 2000.... Equally startling has been the meteoric growth of secularism.... Two immense quasi-religious systems have emerged at the expense of the world's religions: agnosticism... and atheism.... From a minuscule presence in 1900, a mere 0.2 percent of the globe, these systems... are today expanding at the extraordinary rate of 8.5

million new converts each year, and are likely to reach one billion adherents.... A large percentage of their members are the children, grandchildren or great-grandchildren of persons who in their lifetimes were practicing Christians. No Christian strategist in 1900 had envisaged such a massive rate of defection from Christianity within its 19th century heartlands."

Scholars Phil Zuckerman and Gregory Paul say the surge of secularism "has no historical match.... Such a thing has never been seen before." The West is witnessing "the first emergence of mass apostasy in history," they wrote, adding:[4]

"Mass rejection of the gods invariably blossoms in the context of the equally distributed prosperity and education found in almost all First World democracies. There are no exceptions on a national basis.... Every time a nation becomes truly advanced in terms of democratic, egalitarian education and prosperity, it loses the faith. It's guaranteed.... Disbelief now rivals the great faiths in numbers and influence. Never before has religion faced such enormous levels of disbelief, or faced a hazard as powerful as that posed by modernity."

Even President Barack Obama reflects this societal shift. In his 2009 inaugural address, he pointedly declared: "We are a nation of Christians and Muslims, Jews and Hindus - and nonbelievers." It was the first time an American president so boldly ranked doubters equal with believers. Soon afterward, at the annual National Prayer Breakfast, Obama told worshipers:

"I had a father who was born a Muslim but

became an atheist; and grandparents who were non-practicing Methodists and Baptists; and a mother who was skeptical of organized religion, even though she was the kindest, most spiritual person I've ever known."

In February, 2010, another breakthrough occurred as Obama became the first president to invite the skeptic community to the White House for a staff briefing. Leaders of the new-formed Secular Coalition for America conferred with administration chiefs on ways to enforce separation of church and state. Rep. Pete Stark, D-California - the only Congress member to openly question the existence of God - praised the session, saying:

"We cannot accept religious interference in government, whether it's loopholes in child abuse laws for 'faith healing,' or preaching to enlisted members of the military."

A similar breakthrough occurred when Mayor Michael Bloomberg invited New York City Atheists to attend his yearly Interfaith Breakfast on the final day of 2009.

During the 2008 presidential campaign, candidate Obama denounced the puritanical "religious right" for spreading bigotry and attempting to impose fundamentalist strictures on all Americans. "Whatever we once were, we're no longer a Christian nation," he said. "At least, not just. We are also a Jewish nation, a Muslim nation, and a Buddhist nation, and a Hindu nation - and a nation of nonbelievers." He repeated this blunt statement to the Christian Broadcasting Network.

Obama is a master politician, seeking votes from every demographic segment of Americans. He probably figured that around 40 million nonreligious American adults would feel gratitude to him for recognizing them. Further, every survey finds that churchless Americans strongly back the Democratic Party, so it behooves a Democratic president to salute this portion of his base. The Republican Party remains bound to white evangelicals, fundamentalists, Mormons and Pentecostals, so the relentless rise of secularism undercuts the GOP's future.

Growth of American church-avoiders has become too large to ignore. A 2009 nationwide poll by Parade magazine found that only forty-five percent of respondents answered yes to "I consider myself a religious person." Half said they attend worship "never" or "rarely."

Here's another indicator of the culture shift: *The Washington Post*, the flagship newspaper in the nation's capital, has added a "Secularist's Corner" column in which atheist intellectual Susan Jacoby regularly skewers holy nonsense.

Decline of well-educated mainline Protestant denominations has been traumatic - implying that educated Americans no longer need religion. But slippage also is eroding born-again fundamentalism. In a report titled "The Baptists Shrink," the fall 2009 issue of *Religion in the News* said the Southern Baptist Convention, America's largest Protestant body, is losing ground. It quoted convention official Ed Stetzer: "If the 50-year trend continues, projected membership of SBC churches would be 8.7 million in 2050, down from 16.2 million last year."

The SBC's foremost intellectual, Dr. Albert Mohler Jr., president of Southern Baptist Theological Seminary, released a 2009 book,

The Disappearance of God. "The God of the Bible has largely disappeared from view.... Abdication of biblical faith is one of the hallmarks of our age," the theologian says. In his personal blog, he wrote that even the "Christian memory is absent from the lives of millions.... New England, like Europe, is becoming a post-Christian culture.... As New England has followed Europe, will the rest of the nation follow New England?" His book calls for fundamentalist churches to redouble Puritanical attacks on "sin." (But such church intolerance is a major reason why millions of Americans have grown uncomfortable with religion.)

Other fundamentalists bitterly blame intellectuals and "liberals" for religious decline. *The Silencing of God: The Dismantling of America's Christian Heritage* by Alabama churchman Dave Miller protests "the sinister, detrimental transition occurring in our nation." He complains that Christianity is "being systematically jettisoned from our civilization."

Still another evangelical book, *The American Church in Crisis*, by theologian David Olson, warns that church attendance didn't rise in fifteen years, while America's population grew by 52 million.

Privately, many gifted ministers don't believe the supernatural dogmas of their churches. Nobel Prize-winning martyr Martin Luther King Jr. and Coretta Scott King were skeptic-minded Unitarians in Boston before they made a calculated decision to become Deep-South Baptists to fight America's racial segregation. Scholar Robert James Scofield wrote:

"Coretta Scott had been attending Unitarian churches for years before she met and married

Martin, and they both attended Unitarian services while in Boston. He ultimately faced the reality that he would probably not be able to play a role in the civil rights movement in this tradition and thus he became pastor of Dexter Avenue Baptist Church, shortly thereafter being elected to lead the Montgomery bus boycott."[5]

Dr. Scofield noted that many other modern American ministers similarly hold personal beliefs "that they cannot openly preach for fear of losing their congregations."

Legendary Harvard theologian Harvey Cox wrote in 2009 that hard-core fundamentalism, which makes headlines for violence and narrow-minded confrontations, actually is dying around the world. He said:

"A tectonic shift in religion is underway, and the fundamentalist movement is ending.... The very nature of human religiousness is changing in a way inimical to fundamentalist thought.... In Christianity, the fastest-growing wing of the church is the Pentecostal-charismatic [speaking in tongues] wave, which is spreading swiftly around the world, even in mainland China. It now numbers about six hundred million, accounting for one in every four Christians.... The fading of fundamentalism marks a decisive change in global society."[6]

Dr. Cox added: "The modern religious right, the political arm of fundamentalism, foundered on its inability to compromise or build coalitions." Hard-shell believers don't play well with others.

Republican dynamo Sarah Palin spent her life in talking-in-tongues churches - where a visiting African preacher "laid hands" on her to shield her from witches. This type of faith is

69

embraced by a fringe of Americans, but the educated majority sees it as voodoo.

Nobody can predict cultural tides with confidence, yet it seems apparent that America is following Europe on the journey to secularism. Faith remains potent in the United States today, and probably will wield power for generations. But supernatural beliefs have dwindled to near-oblivion in many educated democracies, and America is treading the same path.

One by one, thoughtful Americans follow a course described by Leo Tolstoy in *A Confession*:

"S., a clever and truthful man, once told me the story of how he ceased to believe. On a hunting expedition, when he was already twenty-six, he once, at the place where they put up for the night, knelt down in the evening to pray - a habit retained from childhood. His elder brother, who was at the hunt with him, was lying on some hay and watching him. When S. had finished and was settling down for the night, his brother said to him: 'So you still do that?'

"They said nothing more to one another. But from that day, S. ceased to say his prayers or go to church. And now he has not prayed, received communion, or gone to church, for thirty years. And this not because he knows his brother's convictions and has joined him in them, nor because he has decided anything in his own soul, but simply because the word spoken by his brother was like the push of a finger on a wall that was ready to fall by its own weight. The word only showed that where he thought there was faith, in reality there had long been an empty space, and that therefore the

70

utterance of words and the making of signs of the cross and genuflections while praying were quite senseless actions. Becoming conscious of their senselessness, he could not continue them."

1. Quoted in *The Transcendental Temptation: A Critique of Religion and the Paranormal*, by Paul Kurtz, Prometheus Books, 1991, opening page.

2. *The New York Times*, Oct. 19, 2009, "Good Without God, Atheist Subway Ads Proclaim," by Jennifer B. Lee.

3. CNN.com, Oct. 21, 2009, "Atheist ads to adorn New York subway stations."

4. *The Edge*, 2007, "Why the Gods are Not Winning," by Gregory Paul and Phil Zuckerman.

5. *Tikkun* magazine, November 2009, "King's God: The Unknown Faith of Dr. Martin Luther King Jr.," by Robert James Scofield.

6. *Boston Globe*, Nov. 8, 2009, "Why Fundamentalism will Fail," by Harvey Cox.

(from *Fading Faith*, Gustav Broukal Press, 2010)

Chapter 8

HUMANISTS ARE WINNING, WINNING

When I came of age in the 1950s, deep in Appalachia's Bible Belt, narrow-minded sanctimony prevailed. Here's a recap of former fundamentalist strictures I cited in the opening chapter:

It was a crime for stores to open on the Sabbath.

You could be jailed for looking at something akin to a Playboy magazine or a sexy R-rated movie. Even writing about sex was illegal. My town's righteous mayor sent police to raid bookstores selling "Peyton Place."

It was a felony to be gay. Homosexuals were sent to prison under biblical-sounding "sodomy" laws. (One I recall killed himself to escape that fate.)

It was unthinkable for an unwed couple to live together - and a single girl who had a baby was disgraced, along with her family.

Blacks were banished from white jobs,

neighborhoods and schools. They couldn't enter white-only hotels, restaurants, theaters or swimming pools. The whole culture branded them inferior.

Jews were excluded from various Christian-only clubs.

A desperate girl who terminated a pregnancy faced prison, along with any doctor who helped her.

It was a crime to buy a cocktail or a lottery ticket. Bootleggers and "numbers" runners were nailed by cops.

Mandatory prayer was imposed on school children each day.

Women weren't allowed into most jobs. They couldn't serve on juries. Divorce was hush-hush.

Birth control was illegal in some states, and under-the-counter in mine.

WASPs (white, Anglo-Saxon Protestants) were the only people who mattered - and only staunch churchgoers were deemed respectable.

Evolution drew scant mention in school biology classes, lest it trigger a community uproar.

Looking back, 1950s life now seems unreal, surreal. It's difficult to remember. America couldn't possibly have been so priggish and cruel, you think. But it was.

Today, America has been transformed to an astounding degree. Most of those Puritanical taboos and prejudices gradually fled into the shadows. Now, unwed couples live together freely, and many single females bear babies. Sexual magazines and movies are so unfettered they're practically boring. Gambling ceased being a "sin" and is run by state governments. Women flooded occupations and now earn most college degrees. Prejudice became illegal. Sunday is a whopper shopper day. Gay sex no longer is a crime. School prayer has been banned. Etc.

Why did society evolve? You might say it was because secular humanist values slowly triumphed. Humanists won victory after victory, turning the culture upside down. Bit by bit, religion lost its grip.

Landmark Supreme Court rulings let couples practice birth control in the privacy of their bedrooms - and let black children attend school with whites - and stopped prosecution of writers and photographers who portrayed sex - and allowed women and girls to end pregnancies. The historic civil rights movement toppled this nation's racial apartheid. Congress finally made equality a national policy. The American Civil Liberties Union prevents fundamentalist politicians from imposing worship through government.

In the 2012 national election, voters in three states approved same-sex marriage - and two states authorized recreational pot-puffing - and several open gays were elected to Congress - and America's first black president won reaffirmation. A *Business Week* column called the ballot returns a "liberal landslide."

Of course, all this progress doesn't mean that Utopia has arrived. Die-hard evangelicals still try to stigmatize gays, impose prayer in public events, block teaching of evolution, recriminalize abortion, ban sex from television, etc. Battles of the culture war keep occurring.

Humanism means striving to improve people's lives - and secular means to do so without supernatural religion. Throughout history, secular humanist skeptics have been key figures in struggles for human rights and social justice. Voltaire fought intolerant cruelties of his day. During generations since, unorthodox thinkers crusaded for personal liberties and individual freedoms, while conservatives - especially religious conservatives - resisted each step.

Western society constantly evolves, generally in the direction of more democratic rights. Amid the cacophony of debating groups, freethinking humanists mostly wear the "reformer" label. A few liberal churchgoers also are in the progressive camp, but most churches have defended old moral taboos and narrow prejudices.

Now the good news is that religion is dying in America, as it did in Europe, Canada, Australia, Japan and other advanced democracies. The ratio of secular Americans keeps rising, to 50 million adults and beyond. People who don't attend church are the surest backers of liberal political and social beliefs - the reform urges. Their steady increase portends more progress ahead.

Looking back over my long life, I see a historic parade of victories for secular humanism. They have made America fairer, kinder, more humane, more honest, more decent. And it will be a blessing if humanists continue winning, onward into the future.

(from Free Inquiry, June-July, 2013)

Chapter 9

THE SECULAR AGE

The ratio of incoming American college students with no religion has tripled in the past generation. Each fall, more than 150,000 freshmen arriving at more than 200 schools complete a survey from the Cooperative Institutional Research Program, which asks about many topics. Under "current religious preference," only eight percent marked "none" in 1985 - but the share jumped to 24.6 percent in 2013. The swiftness of this transformation is remarkable.

A century from now, scholars may label our time the dawn of The Secular Age - the long-foretold era when supernatural religion finally faded to a peculiar fringe, mostly ignored. Still more books outline the metamorphosis. For instance:

As early as 1993, *The Culture of Disbelief*, by Yale law professor Stephen L. Carter, declared that America's thinking class "refuses to accept the notion that rational, public-spirited people can take religion seriously." Educated Americans are coming to view "religion as a hobby, trivial and unimportant for serious people, not to be mentioned in serious discourse."

"More and more," he wrote, "our culture seems to take the position that believing deeply in the tenets of one's faith represents a kind of mystical irrationality, something that thoughtful, public-spirited American citizens would do better to avoid."

Recent examples:

Nonbeliever Nation: The Rise of Secular Americans, by lawyer David Niose, president of the American Humanist Association, describes the secular surge as "a major shift in our society." Regarding student doubter groups in schools, he wrote:

"Religious skepticism on college campuses is nothing new, but what's happening today is truly unprecedented. Across all lines of wealth, ethnicity, gender and sexual orientation, students are standing up together to identify as personally secular.... An openly secular life stance, for many young people, is a means of affirmatively taking a position in favor of reason and against ancient superstition."

How the West Really Lost God: A New Theory of Secularization, by Mary Eberstadt, contends that the decline of strong family structure allowed the young to desert churches.

The Great Evangelical Recession: Six Factors That Will Crash the American Church... And How to Prepare, by evangelist John S. Dickerson, warns:

"The church's overall numbers are shrinking. Its primary fuel - donations - is drying up and disappearing. And its political fervor is dividing

78

the movement from within. In addition to these internal crises, the outside host culture is quietly but quickly turning antagonistic and hostile toward evangelicals."

Dickerson cites jolting statistics: 260,000 young American evangelicals leave the faith annually - 2.6 million in the past decade. Two-thirds of Christians in their 20s will depart before age 30. Evangelicals comprise only about eight percent of Americans - not one-third or one-half, as often claimed.

Why Atheism Will Replace Religion: The Triumph of Earthly Pleasures Over Pie in the Sky, by Nigel Barber, asserts that religion fills a need when people are fearful, hungry, ill or endangered - but rising Western prosperity erases the need for faith. He predicts that by 2041, religion in America will slip to minority status, as it already has done in Scandinavia and much of Europe.

The relentless retreat of organized religion has spawned intelligent research by academics - such as creation of the Institute for the Study of Secularism in Society and Culture at Trinity College in Hartford, Connecticut. It publishes a scientific journal, Secularism and Nonreligion.

Some researchers contend that the booming Internet, which lets people around the world share ideas, is a dynamic engine that has boosted the skeptic movement. Other sociologists offer numerous other speculations about what's causing religion to fade in America and the West.

Maybe the answer is simple: Perhaps humanity finally is outgrowing supernatural mumbo-jumbo.

(Note: Subsequent chapters of this book are

varied humanist essays written in recent years.)

PART TWO - SKEPTIC ESSAYS

Chapter 10

THEOLOGY AND HONESTY

My far-flung family is quite diverse. Dr. John F. Haught is a renowned Catholic theologian who has produced a flood of erudite books. A Haught woman in the Southwest wrote several lurid sex novels. And I've churned out a string of skeptic-agnostic books and magazine essays. I once sent both of my relatives a joint note saying our collective writing "shows there are holy Haughts, heathen Haughts and horny Haughts." Neither answered.

Well, Dr. Haught is highly esteemed as a

pinnacle of "sophisticated" theology, a penetrating thinker who probes the divine through abstruse logic beyond the grasp of average folks. His writings carry weight in the most prestigious journals. But when I try to follow his messages, they seem goofy.

Lately, he has attempted to prove that survival-of-the-fittest evolution presents a "grand drama" orchestrated by God. All the ruthless slaughter of prey by predators, all the mass starvation of desperate victims who lose their food supply, even the extinction of 99 percent of all species that ever lived - are part of "an evolutionary drama that has been aroused, though not coercively driven, by a God of infinite love," he wrote in *The Washington Post* .[1]

He added: "Darwin's ragged portrait of life is not so distressing after all. Theologically understood, biological evolution is part of an immense cosmic journey into the incomprehensible mystery of God."

Got that? God is incomprehensible - yet theology is sure his "infinite love" spawned nature's slaughterhouse of foxes ripping rabbits apart, sharks gashing seals, pythons crushing pigs and the rest of the "grand drama of life."

What evidence supports this peculiar conclusion? None - just trust theology.

More recently, Dr. Haught asserted that "critical intelligence" is woven into the universe, not merely in humans.[2] Again, no evidence is offered.

I've decided that there is no such thing as sophisticated theology. Abstruse concepts - for example, "process theology," which declares that God is evolving, nurtured by human responses to him - are just mental houses of cards built by over-thinkers.

At bottom, the issue is simple: Either supernatural spirits exist, or they don't. Either heavens, hells, gods, devils, saviors, miracles and the rest are real, or they're concoctions of the human imagination.

It boils down to honesty: A truthful person shouldn't claim to know things he or she doesn't know. Theologians are in the business of declaring "truths" that nobody possibly could prove. They do so without evidence. In contrast, an honest individual admits: I don't know.

Years ago, as a young newspaper reporter, I encountered theology when I covered the heresy trial of Episcopal Bishop James Pike of California. Actually, it was a pre-trial. Heresy charges had been lodged against him because he doubted the miraculous Virgin Birth, the miraculous Incarnation of God into Jesus, the mystical Trinity, etc. The National House of Bishops met at Wheeling, West Virginia, in 1966 to weigh the charges. During the session, Pike mostly hung out with us newshounds, making wisecracks - not debating holy gobbledygook with fellow bishops. In the end, the church waffled. Pike was censured and charges were sidelined without a heresy inquisition. I guess the bishops didn't want to be laughingstocks in a replay of something akin to the 1925 Scopes Monkey Trial.

Around America, lofty universities pay handsome salaries to theologians who publish grand treatises on the nature of God - although they have no more proof than did the Aztec priests who said the sun would vanish if they stopped sacrificing human victims to an invisible feathered serpent.

One big-time university theologian came from my city, Charleston, West Virginia. Dr. Thomas Jonathan Jackson Altizer - named for his ancestor, General Thomas "Stonewall" Jackson, who fought for slavery in the Civil War - caused a ruckus when he spawned "God is dead" theology.

Dr. Altizer wrote some things that seemed logical to me: "Every man today who is open to experience knows that God is absent," he said in The Gospel of Christian Atheism. That's true enough. God seems absent, as far as any rational observer can tell.

However, Altizer concocted a bizarre scenario: God formerly existed and created the universe, he said - but God decided to terminate himself by entering into Jesus, then dying on a cross and ceasing to exist. Hence, God is dead.

This peculiar theology caused a storm in the 1960s. Fundamentalists raged. Time magazine wrote cover stories. Dr. Altizer received Christian hate mail and death threats. Today, he's retired in Pennsylvania, occasionally giving theology lectures.

Well, his theology is interesting - like that of the Aztecs and their invisible feathered serpent. But I figure they both have little to do with reality.

Thomas Jefferson refused to let theology be taught at his new University of Virginia. He considered theological assertions to be "unintelligible abstractions... absolutely beyond the comprehension of the human mind."[3] He ridiculed the Trinity concept "that three are one, and one is three; and yet that the one is not three, and the three are not one."[4]

Edgar Allan Poe wrote: "After reading all that has been written, and after thinking all that can be thought, on the topics of God and the soul, the man who has a right to say that he thinks at all will find himself face to face with the conclusion that, on these topics, the most profound thought is that which can be the least easily distinguished from the most superficial sentiment."[5]

Ambrose Bierce wrote: "Theology is a thing of unreason altogether, an edifice of assumption and dreams, a superstructure without a substructure."[6]

Legendary newspaperman H.L. Mencken wrote: "There is no possibility whatsoever of reconciling science and theology, at least in Christendom. Either Jesus rose from the dead or he didn't. If he did, then Christianity becomes plausible; if he did not, then it is sheer nonsense."[7]

Of course, like every human phenomenon, religion should be studied by sociologists and psychologists. But theology itself consists of assertions about spirits. I can't imagine why universities consider it a worthy field of scholarship.

1. Haught: *Washington Post*, On Faith, Dec. 2, 2009

2. Haught: "Death" essay posted on Paying Attention to the Sky, March 10, 2011

3. Jefferson: Letter to Archibald Cary, 1816

4. Jefferson: Letter to John Adams, Aug. 22, 1813

5. Poe: *Marginalia*, 1844-49

6. Bierce: Collected Works, 1912

7. Mencken: *Minority Report*, 1956

(from *Free Inquiry* - February-March, 2014)

Chapter 11

THE CRISTERO WAR

In the vast annals of faith-based killing, some episodes are widely known, while other religious bloodbaths are oddly forgotten.

The whole world is aware of the stunning "martyr" attack of Sept. 11, 2001. And most people recall the Jonestown tragedy and the Waco siege - as well as historic horrors: the Inquisition, the witch-hunts, the Crusades, the Reformation wars, the pogroms against Jews, the era of human sacrifice, etc.

However, some other faith-driven tragedies have mostly vanished from public awareness. For example, few Americans know that Catholic-Protestant strife caused a cannon battle in the streets of Philadelphia in 1844. Or that the Taiping Rebellion - led by a mystic who said he was God's second son after Jesus, with a divine mandate to "destroy demons" - killed millions of Chinese in the 1850s.

Here's another half-forgotten holy war: the Cristero conflict that killed 90,000 Mexicans in the 1920s.

It culminated a long, convoluted, gory story spanning a century. It was a classic example of the age-old struggle between reformers and the priest class which gains power in a society, entrenches itself with rulers, lives off the populace, and imposes strictures on the people.

The Cristero War showed the power of religion to propel believers into bloodshed. And it showed that attempts to suppress religion by law can trigger violent "blowback."

After Mexico won independence from Spain in 1821, democracy advocates sought to loosen the Roman Catholic Church's grip on Mexican society. Some anticlerical laws were passed, but they were revoked by dictator Santa Anna in 1834.

Then liberal Benito Juarez, a Zapotec Indian, came to power in the 1850s and enacted La Reforma, a sweeping plan for secular democracy. Among various reforms, it ended Catholicism's exclusive role as the state religion, curtailed the church's great land wealth, halted ecclesiastical courts, abolished church burial fees, and revoked priestly control of education, marriage and other facets of daily life.

The changes were written into a new constitution - but the church excommunicated all Mexican officials who swore to uphold it. Civil war erupted, and religious conservatives seized Mexico City, driving the liberal government to Veracruz. The United States supported Juarez, and his regime defeated the rebels in 1861.

Exiled Mexican conservatives appealed to Catholic France, Catholic Spain and the pope, plus other Europeans. French, Spanish and some English forces invaded Mexico, driving Juarez to the north. A Habsburg noble, Maximilian, was installed as emperor - but he was slow to revoke the anticlerical laws. The clergy and the pope's emissary felt betrayed. Europeans withdrew their military backing. Juarez regrouped, defeated Maximilian's militia, and executed the emperor in 1867.

After Juarez died, successors added further church-state separation. Religious oaths were banned in courts. Church ownership of land was forbidden. But dictator Porfirio Diaz seized power in an 1876 revolt, and gradually restored Catholic privileges during his long reign.

After 1900, young radicals began calling for the overthrow of Diaz, plus distribution of land to peasants and abolition of priestly power. Their unrest finally exploded in the Mexican Revolution that raged from 1910 to 1916. Then the victorious reformers drafted a 1917 constitution mandating democracy - and imposing tough limits on the clergy. It halted church control of schools. It banned monastic orders. It eliminated religious processions and outdoor masses. It again curtailed church ownership of property. And it forbade priests to wear clerical garb, vote, or comment on public affairs in the press.

At first, this strong crackdown was only lightly enforced, and church protests were subdued. But in 1926, new President Plutarco Calles intensified the pressure. He decreed a huge fine (equal to $250 U.S. dollars at the time) on any priest who wore a clerical collar, and demanded five years in prison for any priest who criticized the government.

In response, Catholic bishops called for a

boycott against the government. Catholic teachers refused to show up at secular schools. Catholics refused to ride public transportation. Other civil disobedience occurred. The pope in Rome approved the resistance. The government reacted by closing churches. Ferment grew.

On July 31, 1926, the bishops halted all worship services in Mexico. Today, an ardent Catholic website, *The Angelus*, says the step was unprecedented in Catholic history, and presumably was "intended to push the Mexicans to revolt."

It worked. On Aug. 23, 1926, about 400 armed Catholics barricaded themselves in a Guadalajara church and fought a gunbattle with federal troops, costing 18 lives. The following day, soldiers stormed a Sahuayo church, killing its priest and vicar.

Catholic rebellions erupted in numerous places. Rene Garza, leader of the Mexican Association of Catholic Youth, called for general insurrection, declaring that "the hour of victory belongs to God." Volunteer bands attacked federal facilities and army posts, shouting "Long live Christ the king! Long live the Virgin of Guadalupe!" The rebels called themselves Cristeros - fighters for Christ.

Mexican bishops refused to oppose the rebellion, and quietly approved it. Two priests became guerrilla commanders. One, Aristeo Pedroza, was prim and moral. The other, Jose Vega, was a drinker and womanizer. Three other priests became gunfighters. Many others became covert activists.

Father Vega led a raid on a train, and his brother was killed in the attack. In revenge, the priest had the train cars doused with gasoline and torched, killing 51 civilian passengers inside. The massacre soured public support for the uprising. The government expelled Catholic bishops from the country. After another engagement, Vega ordered all federal prisoners stabbed to death, to save ammunition. The priest later was killed in a raid.

An estimated 50,000 Catholic men became guerrillas, and thousands of Catholic women joined "St. Joan of Arc" support brigades. The rebels began defeating federal units, and controlled large sections of Mexico. Some Catholic army officers mutinied in behalf of the religious insurgents.

The U.S. ambassador to Mexico launched negotiations to end the conflict. His effort was damaged, however, because President Calles was scheduled to be succeeded by moderate President-elect Alvaro Obregon - but a Catholic fanatic assassinated Obregon.

Eventually, talks brought a cease-fire. The Catholic Church was allowed to keep its buildings, and priests were allowed to live in them.

The Cristero War took about 90,000 lives: 56,882 on the government side, plus some 30,000 Cristeros, plus civilians.

On May 21, 2000, the Vatican conferred sainthood on 23 Cristero figures: 20 priests and three laymen. (Normally, each canonization requires evidence of at least two miracles, but the church lowers this standard for "martyrs," so the number of proclaimed miracles in the Cristero War may be less than 46.) On Nov. 20, 2005, thirteen others were designated martyrs and beatified, advancing toward sainthood.

On the government side, no glories were proclaimed for those who struggled and won at least a partial victory against domination by the clergy.

For freethinkers, the message of the Cristero War is clear: Religion is dangerous, laced with the potential for violence (as evidenced by deadly 2006 Muslim eruptions over European cartoons of the Prophet). Over-strong governmental attempts to subdue it can impel believers into irrational slaughter. A wiser course is to maintain separation of church and state, patiently waiting for advances in education and science to erode public support for supernaturalism.

(from *Free Inquiry*, April-May, 2007)

Chapter 12

EVERYONE DOUBTS - OTHER RELIGIONS

Religion is a touchy topic. Church members often become angry if anyone questions their supernatural dogmas. (Bertrand Russell said this is because they subconsciously sense that their beliefs are irrational.) So I try to avoid confrontations that can hurt feelings. Nearly everyone wants to be courteous.

But sometimes disputes can't be avoided. If you think the spirit realm is imaginary, and if honesty makes you say so, you may find yourself under attack. It has happened to many doubters. Thomas Jefferson was called a "howling atheist." Leo Tolstoy was called an "impious infidel."

Well, if you wind up in a debate, my advice is: Try to be polite. Don't let tempers flare, if you can help it. Appeal to your accuser's intelligence.

I've hatched some questions you may find useful. They're designed to show that church members, even the most ardent worshipers, are skeptics too - because they doubt every magical system except their own. If a churchman berates you, perhaps you could reply like this:

You're an unbeliever, just like me. You doubt many sacred dogmas. Let me show you:

-- Millions of Hindus pray over statues of Shiva's penis. Do you think there's an invisible Shiva who wants his penis prayed over - or are you a skeptic?

-- Mormons say that Jesus came to America after his resurrection. Do you agree - or are you a doubter?

-- Florida's Santeria worshipers sacrifice dogs, goats, chickens, etc., and toss their bodies into waterways. Do you think Santeria gods want animals killed - or are you skeptical?

-- Muslim suicide bombers who blow themselves up are taught that "martyrs" go instantly to a paradise full of lovely female houri nymphs. Do you think the bombers now are in heaven with houris - or are you a doubter?

-- Unification Church members think Jesus visited Master Moon and told him to convert all people as "Moonies." Do you believe this sacred tenet of the Unification Church?

-- Jehovah's Witnesses say that, any day now, Satan will come out of the earth with an army of demons, and Jesus will come out of the sky with an army of angels, and the Battle of Armageddon will kill everyone on earth except Jehovah's Witnesses. Do you believe this

94

solemn teaching of their church?

-- Aztecs skinned maidens and cut out human hearts for a feathered serpent god. What's your stand on invisible feathered serpents? Aha! - just as I suspected, you don't believe.

-- Catholics are taught that the communion wafer and wine magically become the actual body and blood of Jesus during chants and bell-ringing. Do you believe in the "real presence" - or are you a disbeliever?

-- Faith-healer Ernest Angley says he has the power, described in the Bible, to "discern spirits," which enables him to see demons inside sick people, and see angels hovering at his revivals. Do you believe this religious assertion?

-- The Bible says people who work on the sabbath must be killed: "Whosoever doeth any work in the sabbath day, he shall surely be put to death" (Exodus 31:15). Should we execute Sunday workers - or do you doubt this scripture?

-- At a golden temple in West Virginia, saffron-robed worshipers think they'll become one with Lord Krishna if they chant "Hare Krishna" enough. Do you agree - or do you doubt it?

-- Members of the Heaven's Gate commune said they could "shed their containers" (their bodies) and be transported to a UFO behind the Hale-Bopp Comet. Do you think they're now on that UFO - or are you a skeptic?

-- During the witch-hunts, inquisitor priests tortured thousands of women into confessing that they blighted crops, had sex with Satan, etc. - then burned them for it. Do you think the church was right to enforce the Bible's command, "Thou shalt not suffer a witch to live" (Exodus 22:18) - or do you doubt this scripture?

-- Members of Spiritualist churches say they talk with the dead during their worship services. Do you think they actually communicate with spirits of deceased people?

-- Millions of American Pentecostals spout "the unknown tongue," a spontaneous outpouring of sounds. They say it's the Holy Ghost, the third god of the Trinity, speaking through them. Do you believe this sacred tenet of many Americans?

-- Scientologists say each human has a soul which is a "Thetan" that came from another planet. Do you believe their doctrine - or doubt it?

-- Ancient Greeks thought a multitude of gods lived on Mt. Olympus - and some of today's New Agers think invisible Lemurians live inside Mt. Shasta. What's your position on mountain gods - belief or disbelief?

-- In the mountains of West Virginia, some people obey Christ's farewell command that true believers "shall take up serpents" (Mark 16:18). They pick up rattlers at church services. Do you believe this scripture, or not?

-- India's Thugs thought the many-armed goddess Kali wanted them to strangle human sacrifices. Do you think there's an invisible goddess who wants people strangled - or are you a disbeliever?

-- Tibet's Buddhists say that when an old Lama dies, his spirit enters a baby boy who's

96

just being born somewhere. So they remain leaderless for a dozen years or more, then they find a boy who seems to have knowledge of the old Lama's private life, and they annoint the boy as the new Lama (actually the old Lama in a new body). Do you think that dying Lamas fly into new babies, or not?

-- In China in the 1850s, a Christian convert said God appeared to him, told him he was Jesus' younger brother, and commanded him to "destroy demons." He raised an army of believers who waged the Taiping Rebellion that killed as many as 20 million people. Do you think he was Christ's brother - or do you doubt it?

Etc., etc. You get the picture.

I'll bet there isn't a church member anywhere who doesn't think all those supernatural beliefs are goofy - except for the one he believes.

You see, by going through a laundry list of theologies, I think you can establish that the average Christian doubts ninety-nine percent of the world's holy dogmas. But the one percent he believes is really no different than the rest. It's a system of miraculous claims, without any reliable evidence to support it.

So, if we can show people that some sacred "truths" are nutty, maybe subconscious logic will seep through, and they'll realize that if some magical beliefs are irrational, all may be.

This progression is rather like a scene in the poignant Peter de Vries novel, The Blood of the Lamb. A gushy woman compliments a Jew because "your people" reduced the many gods of polytheism to just one god. The man replies

97

dourly: "Which is just a step from the truth."

Meanwhile, it's encouraging to realize that almost everyone in the world is a skeptic - at least about other people's religion.

(Talk to Campus Freethought Alliance chapter - reprinted in book, *Everything You Know About God is Wrong*, Disinformation, 2007)

Chapter 13

ERA OF THE HOLY HUMAN BOMB

Abruptly, on Sept. 11, 2001, people around the planet realized that a terrible new phase of human slaughter had arrived. Muslim suicide bombings had been occurring sporadically for two decades, drawing temporary public attention, but the historic 9-11 attack jolted the world into seeing that Islamic self-martyrdom had become the worst menace of the twenty-first century.

Most Westerners were baffled. Why did nineteen young men want to kill thousands of defenseless strangers who had done them no harm? Why did they willingly sacrifice their own lives to hijack four airliners and turn them into weapons of mass destruction? While they lived in America to plan the mass murder, why didn't they feel empathy for surrounding people and families, but instead felt only a compulsion to kill them?

The best clue to the killers' motive is found in their own rallying call, a handwritten

99

exhortation found in their luggage after the horror. Over and over, it beseeched the zealots to kill for God and give their lives gladly, confident that they would be transported to a magical heaven where each would enjoy an allotment of adoring virgins. Here are a few passages, translated from Arabic:

"When the taxi takes you to the airport, remember God constantly.... Smile and be calm, for God is with the believers, and the angels protect you.... And say, 'Oh Lord, take Your anger out on them, and we ask You to protect us from their evils.' And say, 'Oh Lord, block their vision from in front of them, so that they may not see.'... God will weaken the schemes of the non-believers....

"Be happy, optimistic, calm, because you are heading for a deed that God loves and will accept. It will be the day, God willing, that you spend with the women of paradise.... Remember that this a battle for the sake of God, as He said in His book: 'Oh Lord, pour Your patience upon us and make our feet steadfast to give us victory over the infidels....

"Know that the gardens of paradise are waiting for you in all their beauty, and the women of paradise are waiting, calling out, 'Come hither, friend of God.' They have dressed in their most beautiful clothing.... Remind your brothers that this act is for Almighty God."

Astounding! They saw Americans only as "infidels," and they believed that killing infidels along with themselves would guarantee them eternal pleasure with houri nymphs. They were driven by adolescent male sex fantasies, plus heaven-seeking. It was mass murder as a route to paradise.

The terrorists obeyed a fatwa (holy edict) issued in 1998 by Osama bin Laden, which said in part: "We call on every Muslim who believes in God and hopes for reward to obey God's command to kill the Americans and plunder their possessions.... Launch attacks against the armies of the American devils and against those who are allied with them among the helpers of Satan."

What idiocy. Only sickos think there's a God who wants them to kill people.

The 9-11 tragedy wasn't unique. Throughout history, twisted, fermented, supernatural beliefs have caused a wide variety of horrors - from human sacrifice to the Crusades, from the Inquisition to holy wars, from witch-burnings to bloody pogroms, from Jonestown to the David Koresh compound, from nerve gas planted in Tokyo subways by cultists to salmonella planted in Oregon restaurant salad bars by different cultists. Murders at abortion clinics are part of the spectrum. To varying extent, so are assassinations in Ulster, religious riots in India and religio-ethnic warfare that destroyed Yugoslavia.

England still celebrates Guy Fawkes Day to mark the thwarting of a 1605 Catholic plot to blow up Protestants in Parliament. America's tragedy was vastly worse, making Sept. 11 another anniversary reminding humanity to beware of the ghastly mix of religion and hate.

Religious suicide attacks have a spotty history. Ten centuries ago, the Assassin cult sent True Believers on one-way missions to stab rulers to death. Then self-martyrdom faded until recent times. In 1984, Sikh guards decided

101

to become martyrs after they saw a falcon and deemed it a holy omen. They killed Prime Minister Indira Gandhi, whereupon other guards gunned them down. Indira's son, Rajiv, likewise became a victim. A Hindu woman member of the Tamil Tigers of Sri Lanka exploded herself and the prime minister and sixteen others in 1991, because the Tigers felt betrayed by India.

Gradually, suicide attacks became a hallmark of militant Muslims. In the spring of 1983, a bomber blew up his van outside the U.S. Embassy in Beirut, killing sixty-two. That fall, another fanatic - grinning ecstatically - crashed an explosive-filled truck into a U.S. barracks in Beirut, killing 241 Marines, while another killed fifty-eight paratroopers at a French compound. Human bombs also struck in Israel.

In the 1990s, Israel increasingly was ravaged by "martyr bombers" spawned by hopeless desperation among Palestinians trapped in slum-like refugee camps. Young, male, Islamic zealots with explosives hidden under their clothes blew themselves up on crowded buses, in stores, nightclubs, malls, etc., with ghastly effect.

Bombings in 1998 that killed 224 in the U.S. Embassies in Kenya and Tanzania evidently were suicide missions. In 2000, Muslim martyrs from Chechnya detonated four truck bombs simultaneously in four Russian towns, killing fifty-four. Later that year, two others detonated their bomb-laden boat against the USS Cole in a Yemeni harbor, killing seventeen American sailors.

Then 2001 brought the phenomenon to a spectacular peak. History seemed to change when nineteen martyrs turned four U.S. airliners into missiles that killed 3,000

Americans. Three months later, five Muslim suicide volunteers stormed India's Parliament, dying in their attack. Also in 2001, Israel suffered an upsurge, rousing Jews to murderous retaliation.

Since then, volunteer martyrs have become the foremost weapon in this strange new chapter of civilization. Thousands of Muslim self-killings have occurred in numerous nations. Part of the bloodbath has featured Sunni militants blowing up Shiites, or embittered Muslims attacking Islamic governments. The threat is half-invisible, lurking among civilian populations, a menace that can't be defeated by armies, navies and air forces.

The Washington Post reported that 658 suicide attacks happened in 2007 alone, adding: "The bombings have spread to dozens of countries on five continents, killed more than 21,350 people and injured about 50,000 since 1983." Those figures are outdated, boosted by subsequent human bombs.

Time reported that the nature of the suicide bomber has changed: "He used to be easy to describe: male, seventeen to twenty-two years of age, unmarried, unformed, facing a bleak future, fanatically religious and thus susceptible to Islam's promise of a martyr's place in paradise, complete with the affections of heaven's black-eyed virgins. Today's bomber no longer fits the profile."

Now, the magazine said, self-martyrdom has become more popular, drawing eager volunteers, especially among Palestinians humiliated by four decades of Israeli occupation and suppression. Families proudly print newspaper notices announcing "the martyrdom of our son." Pictures of "hero" suicide-killers are worn on T-shirts and key chains. Volunteers include girls such as "Ayat Akhras, eighteen, a straight-A student just months away from graduation and then marriage," Time noted.

Although the Quran forbids suicide, zealot leaders twist language to make it seem that bombers aren't hopeless people taking their own lives, but rather are patriotic warriors against an infidel enemy. "Islam offers potent rationales and rewards for martyrdom," Time said. "In Islam, martyrdom washes away all past sins and guarantees the bomber places for seventy relatives in heaven."

West Virginia political scientist Gerald Beller wrote that a "martyrdom complex" grew among subjugated Palestinians who lost hope after living for decades under military occupation.

Writing in *The Atlantic*, scholar Jonathan Rauch said: "What sets this war apart is its reliance on suicide as an indispensable weapon.... Without its religious element, the current war would be literally inconceivable."

That's the crux: Religion is the deadly fuel causing cruel horror in this new era of the human bomb.

(from *The Charleston Gazette*, Aug. 14, 2002)

104

Chapter 14

RIGHT AND WRONG - A DAILY DILEMMA

Newspapers are different from other news media: In addition to reporting events, we also crusade for causes that seem correct to us. Every day on our editorial page, we preach our view of what's right and wrong on various issues.

But passing moral judgments isn't easy, because right and wrong are elusive. They vary from person to person, place to place, time to time. Confusion and contradiction abound.

Dr. Ed Welch, president of the University of Charleston, wrote a commentary saying moral truths are real and universal. Well, I wouldn't argue with Ed, who holds degrees in both sacred theology and social ethics. But if he worked for a newspaper, up to his ears in daily controversy, he might share my uncertainty.

Look at some examples:

What's the moral truth about abortion? Is it

killing an unborn baby, as fundamentalists say? Or is it rescuing a 14-year-old pregnant girl from a wrecked life? If an abortion is caused by a "morning after" pill, when only a few cells are involved, is there less wrongdoing? In a way, each answer is yes.

My four children all were adopted, so you might think I'd oppose abortion. Yet I feel that every pregnant woman and girl should be allowed to make the painful choice herself. Preachers and politicians shouldn't make it for her. This is the only answer that seems sensible to me.

What's the moral truth about the death penalty? The Old Testament mandated execution of many people, including sabbath workers, disobedient children, gays, non-virgin brides, and many others. But the New Testament said nobody should cast the first stone. I hold the latter view, yet about 80 percent of West Virginians want capital punishment. I can't say that my moral truth is superior to theirs. All I can say is that it's mine.

What about patriotism? Universally, it's considered patriotic for young men to kill each other in war. To me, it's hideous, monstrous. What's the moral truth here?

If there's any universal maxim in all this, it would be something like: Thou shalt not kill - unless politicians tell you to do it in war, or the warden tells you to do it on death row, or doctors tell you to do it at an abortion clinic, or it's self-defense, or it's an accident, etc.

Many other moral dilemmas haunt daily life. When I was a young reporter in the 1950s, homosexuals were sent to prison for "sodomy." Today, being gay isn't a crime. Did moral truth change in the past four decades?

The same question applies to cocktails, lottery tickets and nude magazines or movies. Buying any of those was a crime in the 1950s, and multitudes were jailed on "vice" charges. Now those indulgences all are legal. Was it wrong to jail people for them a half-century ago - or is wrong to wink at transgressors today?

In some states in the 1950s, birth control was illegal. Now it's an inalienable right. Moral truth flip-flopped.

The Holy Koran says God allows Muslim men up to four wives each, and the rich also keep concubines. Polygamy filled the Bible and Mormonism. Yet today's Western laws decree monogamy. Which moral truth should apply to the whole world?

What about private property? If you buy a mountain, are you entitled to cut off the top to get the coal, leaving nature forever marred? Moral standards of coal corporations and environmentalists aren't the same.

Is it immoral for some people to be affluent and well-fed, while others are hungry? If so, America is the most immoral nation, since it's the richest.

The problem with proclaiming a universal truth is that someone, somewhere, lives by an opposing standard. Dr. Welch said stealing is always wrong - which seems true, until you remember that whites stole this continent from the Indians, and felt pious about it.

Personally, I don't think there are fixed answers to moral questions. Views vary with each individual. Your responses depend on your emotional makeup, and who really knows how you acquire it? Our feelings steer us into certain outlooks - liberal or conservative, conformist or rebel, etc. - and then we develop logical reasons to support our inclinations. As Shakespeare said in II Henry IV, the wish is father to the thought.

Life is an onrushing tangle of moral puzzles. History teems with clashing outlooks: the Holy Inquisition against doubters, communism against capitalism, puritans against fun-lovers, labor against management, the power of governments against the rights of individuals.

On our editorial page, we spell out moral stances that seem right to us - but we don't declare that they're universal maxims which everyone should obey.

(from *The Charleston Gazette*, Dec. 10, 1998)

Addendum: In a public newspaper in Appalachia's Bible Belt, I couldn't write the obvious: that moral codes are man-made, not divine. There are no cosmic behavior mandates. The universe doesn't care whether people kill each other, or suffer horrible diseases, or copulate in orthodox manner. Only people are concerned with such topics.

The great Harvard biologist-thinker-scholar Edward O. Wilson summed up perfectly:

"Centuries of debate on the origin of ethics come down to this: Either ethical precepts, such as justice and human rights, are independent of human experience or else they are human inventions.... The split is not, as popularly supposed, between religious believers and secularists. It is between trancendentalists, those who think that moral

108

guidelines exist outside the human mind, and empiricists, who think them contrivances of the mind....

"I will, of course, try to be plain about my own position: I am an empiricist. On religion I lean toward Deism but consider its proof largely a problem in astrophysics. The existence of a cosmological God who created the universe (as envisioned by Deism) is possible, and may eventually be settled, perhaps by forms of material evidence not yet imagined. Or the matter may be forever beyond human reach. In contrast, and of far greater importance to humanity, the existence of a biological God, one who directs organic evolution and intervenes in human affairs (as envisioned by theism) is increasingly contravened by biology and the brain sciences. The same evidence, I believe, favors a purely material origin of ethics.... Ethical precepts and religious faith are entirely material products of the mind...." [1]

If moral laws actually exist apart from human minds, Wilson says, it would have awesome significance.

"If empiricism is disproved, and transcendentalism is compellingly upheld, the discovery would be quite simply the most consequential in human history."

But he's confident that it never will happen. Therefore, right and wrong are human concepts - and people change, from generation to generation, and continent to continent.

1. From *Consilience: The Unity of Knowledge*, by Edward O. Wilson, Alfred A. Knopf, 1998 - chapter 11: Ethics and Religion

Chapter 15

ADVENTURES IN THE BIBLE BELT

For many years, I was *The Charleston Gazette's* religion reporter and, believe me, I met some amazing denizens of Appalachia's Bible Belt.

Does anyone remember Clarence "Tiz" Jones, the evangelist-burglar? Jones had been a West Virginia champion amateur boxer in his youth, but succumbed to booze and evil companions, and spent a hitch in state prison. Then he was converted and became a popular Nazarene revivalist. He roved the state, drawing big crowds, with many coming forward to be saved.

But police noticed a pattern: In towns where Jones preached, burglaries happened. Eventually, officers charged him with a break-in. This caused a backlash among churches. Followers said Satan and his agents were framing the preacher. The Rev. John Hancock, a former *Charleston Daily Mail* reporter turned Nazarene pastor, led a "Justice for Tiz Jones" committee. Protest marches were held.

Then Jones was nabbed red-handed in another burglary, and his guilt was clear. He went back to prison.

Another spectacular West Virginia minister was "Dr." Paul Collett, a faith-healer who claimed he could resurrect the dead - if they hadn't been embalmed. Collett set up a big tent in Charleston and drew multitudes, including many in wheelchairs and on crutches. The healer said he had revived a corpse during a previous stop at Kenova. He urged believers to bring him bodies of loved ones, before embalming.

Collett moved his show into the old Ferguson Theater and broadcast over Charleston radio stations. One night he said a cancer fell onto the stage. Another night, he said he turned water into wine.

I attended a service and wrote a skeptical account - focusing on his many money collections. After the article appeared, 40 of Collett's followers invaded the Gazette newsroom, then on Hale Street. Luckily, it was my day off. The night city editor called police, and also summoned burly printers from the type shop, who backed the throng out the door.

Collett claimed to have 10,000 adherents in Kanawha County. For five years, he collected money to build a 12-doored "Bible Church of All Nations," which was to be "the biggest tabernacle in West Virginia." Then he moved to Canada, leaving not a rack behind.

He returned some years later and preached at a serpent-handling church on Scrabble Creek near Gauley Bridge. (I often wrote about the ardent mountain worshipers who pick up buzzing rattlesnakes and thrust their hands into fire to show their faith. They're earnest and decent people - even though they have a high mortality rate during prayer services.)

The leader of the Scrabble Creek church, Elzie Preast - who never took money from members - began to suspect that Dr. Collett was bilking his congregation. In an Old Testament-type showdown, the two ministers scuffled, one shouting "Manifest him, Lord!" and the other yelling "Rebuke the devil!"

Then Dr. Collett vanished for good. Meanwhile, the serpent churches spawned other tales:

Once a weekly newspaper printed photos of church weddings, including one in which the bride and groom each held a rattler.

Another time, we heard that politicians in a rural county allowed serpent-handlers to meet in the dilapidated courthouse. Some snakes escaped into crevices in the walls - and emerged weeks later, causing bedlam among courthouse employees.

A former University of Charleston sociologist, Dr. Nathan Gerrard, studied the serpent phenomenon. He administered a psychological test to the Scrabble Creek flock, and gave the same test to a nearby Methodist congregation as a control group. The serpent-handlers came out mentally healthier.

Once the great Harvard theologian Harvey Cox accompanied Dr. Gerrard and me to a different serpent church, on Camp Creek in Boone County. When the worshipers began their trancelike "dancing in the spirit," we were surprised to see Dr. Cox leap up and join the hoofing.

112

Later, visiting professors accompanied us to a third serpent church, at Fraziers Bottom, Putnam County. One professor's wife, barely five feet tall, was an opera soprano. The worshipers - whose music usually is the twang of electric guitars - asked her to sing. She stood on the altar rail and trilled an aria from La Boheme while the congregation listened respectfully.

Meanwhile, the parade of colorful evangelists never stopped. One was Charleston faith-healer Henry Lacy, who handed out calling cards saying simply "Lacy the Stranger." He often came into the Gazette newsroom to lay hands on reporters to cure their hangovers.

He once offered to halt a cold wave in West Virginia, if state officials would return his driver's license, which had been confiscated.

And there was roving healer A.A. Allen, who visited West Virginia with jars containing froglike bodies that he said were demons he had cast out of the sick. He vanished after a revival at Wheeling, and was found dead of alcoholism in a San Francisco hotel room with $2,300 in his pocket.

(Marjoe Gortner, the boy evangelist who later confessed that his show was a fraud, said Allen once advised him how to tell when a revival was finished and it was time to go to the next city: "When you can turn people on their head and shake them and no money falls out, then you know God's saying, 'Move on, son.'")

And "the Plastic Eye Miracle," the Rev. Ronald Coyne, visited the Charleston Civic Center. He was a one-eyed evangelist who said a faith-healer had enabled him to see through his artificial eye. Several of us in the audience

113

wrapped tape over his good eye, and he read items aloud, using his empty eye socket. It seemed legitimate, and I was mystified.

Those were heady days in the Bible Belt - before evangelists created million-dollar TV empires and became the ayatollahs of the Republican Party. The holy rovers of yesteryear provided marvelous theater. Today's mountain religion seems pale in comparison.

(from *The Charleston Gazette*, Dec. 7, 1993)

Chapter 16

THE FOREST IS MY CHURCH

A marvelous asset surrounds millions of Americans. Part of the public ignores it, but a significant group cherishes it. I'm talking about the lush forest covering vast regions, including eighty percent of my state, West Virginia.

For woods-lovers, the forest is an enticing lure that's freely available, almost everywhere you look. West Virginia is engulfed in nature, with countless shady trails along deep ravines or winding among tall trees that rise like pillars of a cathedral. Woodland is a place of spiritual contentment, a quiet refuge for calm reflection and long thoughts. It feels like being in church. And forest trekking is healthy, good for fitness as well as inner peace.

For seven decades, I've been hiking the Mountain State's woods. I even make my own trails around Lake Chaweva and other fringes of Charleston. Along my personal paths, the groves and rock formations become private retreats, known like the back of my hand.

When I enter the forest, usually with a companion dog, serenity takes over. Dappled sunlight glimmers and moves with breezes. Silence prevails, except for soft rustling. Wildflowers and ferns sprinkle the forest floor. Far above, the treetop canopy is like a green awning. Squirrels scurry. Deer often appear. Turkeys are rarer. Once I saw a bobcat in Webster County. I've visited beaver ponds in Canaan Valley and near Beech Fork Lake.

Beloved poet Robert Frost said "the woods are lovely, dark and deep," and he was correct.

Trees seem timeless, because their life-and-death cycle is extremely slow. Some cliffs have ancient seashells embedded in rock layers, showing that these hilltops once were ocean floors, long before humans began. They impart a sense of eternity even greater than the lives of trees. Thousands of generations of people have come and gone while those outcrops stood silent.

For years, I hiked with Kanawha Trail Club, often amid the tall timber of Kanawha State Forest. When I grew too old to keep up with the tough veterans, I returned to solitary exploring, mostly with my three-legged boxer. Recently I cleared a path from the Oakridge Drive hilltop through stately woods along an old logging road down to the Kanawha-Charleston animal shelter. It's beautiful.

Hiking through other people's woodland is legal in West Virginia. The state trespass law (Code 61-3B) is hospitable. Unless property is fenced, cultivated or posted with regular signs, anyone may wander at will through open woods. It's completely free and unsupervised.

Good hikers are responsible guests, never littering, and even picking up any rubbish.

West Virginia is ideal for forest-lovers. This state has America's highest ratio of hardwood timber, covering 12 million of the state's 15.4 million acres. Maine and New Hampshire have slightly higher percentage of woodlands, but theirs is mostly evergreens. West Virginia has 47 state parks and forests, plus two national forests and 93 public lakes - most with hiking trails and campsites. As the coal industry shrinks, abandoned spur railways are being converted into free public rail-trails. Even rest areas along interstate highways have small hiking trails.

Hundreds of West Virginia volunteers, groups and agencies cherish the forest as I do and work to make it more hikable. The state Trails Coalition mapped a statewide master network of around 150 public forest paths, or "linear parks," as it calls them. The group hopes to "make West Virginia the 'trails destination' of the eastern United States." The Nature Conservancy welcomes hikers to its 17 Mountain State preserves and landscapes. Outdoors enthusiast Leonard Adkins wrote a book titled Fifty Hikes in West Virginia. The state Scenic Trails Association sponsors the 300-mile Allegheny Trail from Preston to Monroe counties. Many other organizations serve the forest, with volunteer crews tending trails.

Besides all the official designated pathways, endless opportunity for outdoor escape lies in the woods that surrounds nearly every neighborhood.

When my four children were young, we had our own tent-and-campfire site for overnight outings in hills behind Lake Chaweva. One of our trails went directly through a split in bizarre stones we called the Enchanted Rocks. I told children and grandchildren that fairies dance on the formation at night, but they didn't believe me.

We held numerous weenie roasts at another huge rock formation reachable only by a long hike. I've left final instructions: When the time comes, I want my ashes sprinkled around that rock edifice, so I'll have the largest tombstone in West Virginia. There's no better place to end up than in the green sanctuary covering four-fifths of this state.

(from *The Charleston Gazette*, July 18, 2009)

Chapter 17

SEEKERS, NOT FINDERS

I knew a spunky old doctor who held a philosophy discussion circle in her home. Once a month, members gathered to ponder and debate the baffling riddles of existence. Some sessions employed tape recordings or videos by university scholars. When Dr. Henrietta finally had to move into a care home, the group met in an assembly room there. After she died, the circle continued in her name. I've been a member for decades.

Socrates, Aristotle, Baruch Spinoza, David Hume, Immanuel Kant, Friedrich Nietzsche, Jean-Paul Sartre - the deepest thinkers the world has known, who tried to fathom the meaning of life, but never quite unraveled it - were analyzed year after year.

Our sessions are a bit odd, because our talk leader, Dr. Michael Petersen, moved to a hospital job in Wheeling. He calls on a speaker phone, and we debate his disembodied voice. After a moment, we hardly notice that he isn't in the room.

The group includes chemists, physicians, psychologists, housewives - some aging. Most of the members are churchgoers, yet they crave answers beyond church explanations for the profound, baffling questions of existence:

Why is nature so cruel, with hawks killing field mice, sharks ripping seals, foxes devouring rabbits and spiders snaring flies?

Why is the vast universe so violent, with stars exploding into supernovas, and black holes gobbling solar systems?

If the universe has a compassionate creator, why do earthquakes, tornados, volcanos and hurricanes kill thousands of people? Why does leukemia kill children, and breast cancer kill women?

And the ultimate question: Why is anything here, at all?

Session after session, we delve into such insoluble riddles, knowing that we can't find answers, but feeling impelled to keep searching. We're seekers, but not finders. We explore all the "isms" - empiricism, logical positivism, humanism, phenomenalism, scholasticism, idealism, neoplatonism, etc. - including some so long dead that they're "wasms."

Personally, I'm drawn to existentialism: We and the universe exist, but we can't find solid evidence of a cosmic purpose, so we each must form our own values and goals. As Martin Heidegger put it: We are doomed to live and die without really knowing why we are here.

It reminds me of a passage in "Zorba the Greek" in which the burly, uneducated foreman confronts his bookish, intellectual employer one night as they relax after work. It goes like this:

Zorba looked at the sky with open mouth in a sort of ecstasy, as though he were seeing it for the first time....

"Can you tell me, boss," he said, and his voice sounded deep and earnest in the warm night, "what all these things mean? Who made them all? And why? And, above all" - here Zorba's voice trembled with anger and fear - "why do people die?"

"I don't know, Zorba," I replied, ashamed, as if I had been asked the simplest thing, the most essential thing, and was unable to explain it.

"You don't know!" said Zorba in round-eyed astonishment, just like his expression the night I had confessed that I could not dance.... "Well, all those damned books you read - what good are they? Why do you read them? If they don't tell you that, what do they tell you?"

"They tell me about the perplexity of mankind, who can give no answer to the question you've just put to me, Zorba."

The perplexity of mankind - that's the bottom line at the philosophy club.

The old doctor knew that we'd never find ultimate answers. But she knew that the search is rewarding, anyway.

(from *The Charleston Gazette*, Nov. 23, 2002)

Chapter 18

EXISTENTIALISM - FOR SECULAR HUMANISTS

When I came of age in the 1950s, and slowly began to think about life, I developed a strange feeling that the world is senseless, irrational, chaotic.

Forty million people had just been killed in World War II, and everyone said how noble and heroic it was. But the "Big One" was only the latest of thousands of gory wars stretching back before the earliest written records began. The number of wars is impossible to count. Honduras and El Salvador fought a 1969 war over a soccer match. England fought one with Spain in the 1700s because a British ship captain's ear was cut off by Spaniards. I wondered: Is this what people do to each other: send their patriotic young men to kill other young men who feel just as patriotic for the opposite side?

Also, I saw three-fourths of humanity praying to invisible spirits and hoping to go to magical heavens. All politicians invoked the gods. But there's no evidence that any of it is real. I thought: it's crazy to worship something that probably doesn't exist - yet billions of people do it.

I saw breast cancer killing women, and leukemia killing children, and hawks ripping shrieking rabbits, and sharks slashing baby seals, and pythons crushing pigs - and everyone said it was the divine plan of the all-loving, all-merciful Father Creator. Good grief.

I saw the cruel unfairness of life: how some are retarded, or blind, or abruptly ravaged by cancer, or killed by drunken drivers, or dragged down by wasting diseases, or paralyzed by strokes, while others are not. It's an incomprehensible lottery - sheer luck: spin the wheel to see whether you'll have a long, healthy life, or die early in agony.

The universe doesn't care whether we live or die, or whether we're virtuous or sinful. Nature simply doesn't give a damn.

Our very existence is hit-or-miss. Some are born with high I.Q., in privileged white families in our rich modern society, and some are African pygmies in the jungle. I could have been born female, or gay, or black, or with cerebral palsy, or spina bifida - and I wouldn't be the same person at all. And regardless how you're born, we're all doomed to age and sicken and die. That's our only equality.

Our lives are just brief blips in the enormous span of human history. We could have been prehistoric primates - or medieval serfs - or slaves in Dixie - or people centuries in the future - serving our short stays, then gone. Sometimes it boggles me to realize that people during the Crusades, or bubonic plague times, or the American Civil War, tried just as fervently to cope with their daily lives and problems as we do today. Then death erased them.

When a life is over, the question lingers: Was there any point, really? Was it all meaningless? What was achieved by the lifelong hassle of earning money, raising children, fending off illness, and finally succumbing? I guess the answer is: Each person's life is intensely real and vital to him or her while it's in progress - then it ends. Afterward, did it really matter? (I remember a tombstone epitaph: "Where he goes and how he fares, nobody knows and nobody cares.")

More irrationalities: I saw thousands of people pickling their brains with dope - or staggering from alcohol - or sucking tobacco smoke into their lungs - for what purpose? Willfully damaging yourself makes no sense.

Most people seem logical and friendly and honest at a personal level - yet, collectively, many are eager to plunge into war, or ostracize blacks, or shoot harmless deer, or send gays to prison, or get "saved" at revivals. Sometimes I feel like a visitor in a vast lunatic asylum,

baffled as I watch goofy behavior.

That was my confused and bemused condition in the 1950s, when existentialism burst onto the world scene like a tidal wave of new thinking.

It said, yes, life is absurd and ultimately pointless. We find ourselves living lives, but we don't know why we are here. We are doomed to die without ever knowing why we were "thrown into the world." The only thing we have is our own individual lives, which are temporary. We exist - period - which provides the name, existentialism. We are "condemned to be free," to live inside our own minds and skulls, separated from others.

And yet, no matter how much chaos and cruelty are around us, each of us has no choice but to formulate values and decide how we will behave, personally. We must craft an "authentic" life for ourselves, regardless of what the surrounding society does.

(Actually, I'm not sure I swallow existentialism's assertion that we must decide our own values, because I don't know whether people really choose their beliefs. Could I choose to be a racist Klansman in a lynch mob, if I wanted? Could I choose to be an armed robber? Could I choose to be a Pentecostal speaking "the unknown tongue"? Those values are alien to my psyche, so it isn't quite a free choice for me to reject them.)

Once I saw the absurdist play, *Waiting for Godot*, in which nothing really makes sense, nothing is quite understood, everything is confused and uncertain - with patriotic-sounding political language that actually is gibberish - and I thought the play was a brilliant reflection of daily reality. When I was a kid in the 1930s, there was a Gene Ahern comic strip in which a bearded little man always said "Nov shmoz ka pop." Eventually I latched onto it as a marvelous expression of meaninglessness.

Somehow, existentialism seems a perfect philosophy for secular humanists - for nonconformists who can't embrace the majority god-chanting and war-fever chest-thumping

125

and entrenched unfairnesses of society all around them. It's for misfit thinkers who see the world as half-loony, so they each seek a private, personal path, outside the mainstream, trying to be honest and devoted to values that seem right to them alone.

During the 1950s, existentialism captivated me. But maybe I devised my own personal concept of it - my own concoction - not fully meshed with the view of experts. Actually, that's probably the way most secular humanists form their worldviews.

(from *Free Inquiry*, April-May 2013)

Chapter 19

TELLING THE TRUTH

People sometimes ask me whether I'm an agnostic, an atheist, a skeptic - or what. I have a standard reply: I don't think about labels; I just think about being honest and truthful.

Honest people don't claim to know supernatural stuff that nobody can know. Truthful people don't say they're sure of gods, devils, heavens, hells, miracles, saviors and the like, when there's no actual evidence. Ministers who proclaim certainty about invisible, magical things are dishonest, I think.

Years ago, when I was a young news reporter, my city editor was an H.L. Mencken-style cynic who laughed at hillbilly preachers, and I joined him. But as a naïve seeker of wisdom, I worried - so I told him, "OK, you're right that they're spouting fairy tales and mumbo-jumbo, but what's the actual truth? Why are we here? Why is the world here? Why do we live and die? What answer can an honest, sincere, thinking person give?"

He eyed me and replied, "You can say: I don't

127

know." Bingo. That rang a bell in my psyche that I've never forgotten. Admitting that you don't know is truthful. It's just about the only honest stand you can take. Confessing that you cannot answer is moral and honorable.

Later, I realized that an honest person can go further to reach rational conclusions about whether supernatural claims are plausible. You can't really prove that invisible fairies don't dance in the darkness, or that the Virgin Mary doesn't miraculously appear to believers, or that witches don't copulate with Satan, or that the Angel Moroni didn't reveal golden plates and later take them back to heaven, but your intelligence can conclude that such claims are so far-fetched that they should rank with children's fantasy stories.

Therefore, honesty leads you to the secular humanist outlook: to acceptance of scientific evidence as the key to knowledge, plus a determination to strive to help humanity without supernatural aid. Humanism is a belief system that a truthful person can embrace.

Worldwide, the entire species accepts humanism in the sense of wanting to make life better for people, but the humanist movement as an alternative to religion is a smallish crusade led by a few dedicated intellectuals. Most folks never heard of groups like the American Humanist Association or the International Humanist and Ethical Union (IHEU), but those organizations are busy at work, endlessly trying to counteract religious supernaturalism.

Back in the 1980s, some of these groups launched World Humanism Day, observed every June 21 on the summer solstice. Choosing the time of longest daylight was designed to symbolize the light of reason overcoming the darkness of superstition. Each year, some skeptic groups hold parties or ceremonies on June 21.

But the holiday hasn't exactly swept the planet. I had never heard of World Humanist Day until I was asked to give this talk about it.

However, below the radar, humanism truly is sweeping the planet. It began with thinkers in Ancient Greece. Then it revived among intellectuals in the Renaissance, the Enlightenment and the Age of Reason. As the modern scientific age snowballed, religion retreated and secular humanism soared. The *World Encyclopedia of Christianity* says, "The number of nonreligionists... throughout the 20th century has skyrocketed from 3.2 million in 1900, to 697 million in 1970, and on to 918 million in A.D. 2000."

We're living in the long-predicted Secular Era. Religion is dying. Humanism is the value system fitting the new epoch. The IHEU gives this definition:

"Humanism is a democratic and ethical life stance that affirms that human beings have the right and responsibility to give meaning and shape to their own lives. It stands for the building of a more humane society through an ethics based on human and other natural values in a spirit of reason and free inquiry through human capabilities. It is not theistic, and it does not accept supernatural views of reality."

One dictionary defines humanism as "seeking, without religion, the best in, and for, human beings." Another calls it "a doctrine, attitude or way of life centered on human interests or values; especially, a philosophy that usually rejects supernaturalism and stresses an individual's dignity and worth and capacity for self-realization through reason." Still another says it's "the rejection of religion in favor of the advancement of humanity by its own efforts."

And the *Oxford Companion to Philosophy* says humanism is "an appeal to reason in contrast to revelation or religious authority as a means of finding out about the natural world and destiny of man, and also giving a grounding for morality.... Humanist ethics is also distinguished by placing the end of moral action in the welfare of humanity rather than in fulfilling the will of God."

So - happy World Humanist Day!

(from *Humanist Network News* - June 20, 2012)

Chapter 20

AGOG OVER GOG AND MAGOG

 Incredibly, President George W. Bush told French President Jacques Chirac in early 2003 that Iraq must be invaded to thwart Gog and Magog, the Bible's satanic agents of the Apocalypse.

Honest. This isn't a joke. The president of the United States, in a top-secret phone call to a major European ally, asked for French troops to join American soldiers in attacking Iraq as a mission from God.

Now out of office, Chirac recounts that the American leader appealed to their "common faith" (Christianity) and told him:

"Gog and Magog are at work in the Middle East.... The biblical prophecies are being fulfilled.... This confrontation is willed by God, who wants to use this conflict to erase his people's enemies before a New Age begins."

This bizarre - seemingly deranged - episode

happened while the White House was assembling its "coalition of the willing" to unleash the Iraq invasion. Chirac says he was boggled by Bush's call, and "wondered how someone could be so superficial and fanatical in their beliefs."

After the 2003 call, the puzzled French leader didn't comply with Bush's request. Instead, his staff asked Thomas Romer, a theologian at the University of Lausanne, to analyze the weird appeal. Dr. Romer explained that the Old Testament book of Ezekiel contains two chapters (38 and 39) in which God rages against Gog and Magog, sinister and mysterious forces menacing Israel. Jehovah vows to smite them savagely, to "turn thee back, and put hooks into thy jaws," and slaughter them ruthlessly. In the New Testament, the mystical book of Revelation envisions Gog and Magog gathering nations for battle, "and fire came down from God out of heaven, and devoured them."

In 2007, Dr. Romer recounted Bush's strange behavior in Lausanne University's review, *Allez Savoir.* A French-language Swiss newspaper, *Le Matin Dimanche*, printed a sarcastic account titled: "When President George W. Bush saw the prophesies of the Bible coming to pass." France's *La Liberte* likewise spoofed it under the headline, "A small scoop on Bush, Chirac, God, Gog and Magog." But other news media missed the amazing report.

Subsequently, ex-President Chirac confirmed the nutty event in a long interview with French journalist Jean-Claude Maurice, who tells the tale in his new book, *Si Vous le Répétez, Je Démentirai* (If You Repeat it, I Will Deny), released by the publisher Plon.

Oddly, mainstream media are ignoring this alarming revelation that Bush may have been half-cracked when he started his Iraq war. My own paper, *The Charleston Gazette* in West Virginia, is the only U.S. newspaper to report it, so far. Canada's *Toronto Star* recounted the story, calling it a "stranger-than-fiction disclosure... which suggests that apocalyptic fervor may have held sway within the walls of the White House." Fortunately, on-line commentary sites are spreading the news, filling the press void.

The French revelation fits with other known aspects of Bush's renowned evangelical certitude. For example, a few months after his phone call to Chirac, Bush attended a 2003 summit in Egypt. The Palestinian foreign minister later said the American president told him he was "on a mission from God" to defeat Iraq. At that time, the White House called this claim "absurd."

Recently, *GQ* magazine revealed that former Defense Secretary Donald Rumsfeld attached warlike Bible verses and Iraq battle photos to war reports he hand-delivered to Bush. One declared: "Put on the full armor of God, so that when the day of evil comes, you may be able to stand your ground."

It's awkward to say openly, but now-departed President Bush is a religious crackpot, an ex-drunk of small intellect who "got saved." He never should have been entrusted with power to start wars.

For six years, Americans really haven't known why he launched the unnecessary Iraq attack. Official pretexts turned out to be baseless. Iraq had no weapons of mass destruction, after all, and wasn't in league with terrorists, as the White House alleged. Collapse of his asserted reasons led to speculation about hidden motives: Was the invasion loosed to gain control of Iraq's oil - or to protect Israel - or to complete Bush's father's old vendetta against the late dictator Saddam Hussein? Nobody ever found an answer.

Now, added to the other suspicions, comes the goofy possibility that abstruse, supernatural, idiotic, laughable, Bible prophecies were a factor. This casts an ominous pall over the needless war that has killed more than 4,000 young Americans and cost U.S. taxpayers perhaps $1 trillion.

Allez Savoir - September 2007

Le Matin Dimanche - Sept. 9, 2007

La Liberte - Sept. 17, 2007

Si Vous le Repetez, Je Dementirai - March 2009, Plon publisher

The Charleston Gazette - May 28, 2009

Toronto Star - May 29, 2009

(and now 4,240 Web sites contain the report, according to Bing)

(from *Free Inquiry* - Aug/Sept 2009)

Chapter 21

HOLY HORROR: THE TAIPINGS

History awareness is woefully spotty. Everyone knows that World War II killed perhaps 40 million people - but few ever heard of a bizarre religious war that inflicted similar slaughter.

China's Taiping Rebellion in the mid-1800s was the bloodiest civil war in human history, and possibly the worst conflict of any type, depending on whose casualty estimate you accept. Most historians tally the death toll at 20 million, but some speculate 50 million or 100 million, largely stemming from war-caused famines and epidemics.

The weird uprising began because a Chinese man, Hong Xiuquan, read Christian missionary pamphlets, then said he experienced a vision in which God told him he was a younger brother of Jesus (apparently forming a Holy Quaternary: father, two sons and Holy Ghost). Hong said God commanded him to "destroy demons," meaning officials and supporters of the reigning Qing Dynasty.

Hong proclaimed the "Heavenly Kingdom of Peace" (Taiping Tianguo), and began raising a volunteer army to wage the opposite of peace. Oppressed peasants in southern China flocked to him, partly because of his miracle message and partly because they felt bitterness against the ruthless northern Qing government.

Early rebel victories against Qing troops in 1850 caused the Taiping army to swell beyond 700,000. One of leader Hong's top aides - Yang Xiuqing, who claimed that his utterances were the voice of God speaking through him - became a secondary commander. Together, they mandated a puritanical society inflicting the death penalty for various vices and imposing strict separation of sexes. Although polygamy was banned, Hong, the supposed younger brother of Jesus, had a harem of concubines.

In March, 1853, the Taipings conquered Nanking, killing 30,000 imperial troops and civilians. Hong renamed the city "Heavenly Capital" and built his "Palace of Heavenly King" there.

The rebellion mushroomed, and so did the horrendous death toll. The Taipings soon controlled much of south-central China, about one-fourth of the nation and nearly half of the population. Visionary Hong partly withdrew as military commander - but he grew suspicious of aide Yang's pronouncements as the "voice of God." He ordered execution of Yang and his family in 1856, along with extermination of Taiping soldiers loyal to Yang.

Qing Dynasty rulers struggled to defeat the snowballing mutiny. Several local resistance militias were organized. The largest was the "Ever-Victorious Army" led by American commander Frederick Ward. After Ward was killed in 1862, command was taken by Briton Charles "Chinese" Gordon. Hiring expert foreign commanders for local mercenary defense armies was expedient during that chaotic period in China.

Gradually, the Taipings were beaten backward. But many stubbornly fought to the death. Eventually, they were surrounded in their capital, Nanking. Hong relinquished power to his 15-year-old son. Then Hong died of food poisoning from unclean vegetables in the starving city. As imperial troops overran Nanking in July 1864, many Taipings took poison and others suffered mass execution. The final battle killed 100,000 in three days.

Hong's body was exhumed and burned, and his ashes were blasted from a cannon, to deprive fanatical followers of a gravesite where he could be worshipped as a divine martyr.

Several hundred thousand Taiping soldiers remained in surrounding regions, and continued guerrilla resistance until 1871.

Footnote: Unlucky Chinese Gordon later was afflicted by murderous religion a second time. In 1885, he led Egyptian defenses against a Muslim holy war in the upper Nile valley, and was killed when the fanatics overran Khartoum.

(from *Free Inquiry*, Oct-Nov 2012)

Chapter 22

RELIGION'S BUCKET LEAKS LIKE A SIEVE

The worst aspect of Christianity is that it makes no sense - and most of its 2.2 billion believers around the planet cannot see the illogic. Let me explain:

More than any other faith, Christianity teaches that an all-loving, all-merciful, all-powerful, benevolent father-creator made the universe and everything it contains. Ministers focus on God's special fatherly love for his favorites, people.

But if a supernatural spirit made everything, he also made breast cancer that kills women, leukemia that ravages children, brain tumors, malaria, tapeworms, spina bifida, Down's syndrome, flesh-eating bacteria and many other torments that sicken or kill his human offspring. Further, he must have made tornados, earthquakes, hurricanes, volcanoes, floods and sundry disasters that mangle and maim great masses of people. Remember the 2004 Indian Ocean tsunami that drowned

200,000, mostly children? Did "our father which art in heaven" just watch as a spectator?

How many desperate parents pray fervently for God to save their cancer-stricken children - to no avail? Their anguished hopes find only silence.

In addition to this cruelty toward people, the animal kingdom that the loving creator supposedly made - "every living creature that moveth" - is a hell of killing and eating. Tennyson wrote of "nature, red in tooth and claw."[1] Did you know that rabbits scream when ripped by a fox's fangs? I heard it once, and I still feel my shudder. Also, with my grandchildren, I put corn in trees for squirrels - until a hawk swooped away with a muncher.

Mark Twain wrote: "The spider kills the fly, and eats it; the bird kills the spider, and eats it; the wildcat kills the goose; the - well, they all kill each other. It is murder all along the line."[2]

Some insects even plant their eggs inside others, so the hatching offspring can devour the hosts alive, from within. If a mighty Intelligent Designer devised all these things, he's a monster, not a merciful father. No human would be so cruel. Why would anyone worship such a vicious creator - and insist that the heavenly father is Pure Love? See what I mean about illogic?

Rationality doesn't rule out a malicious, sadistic creator-god, but it definitely scuttles the possibility of a merciful one. In philosophy, this inescapable conclusion is called the "problem of evil." It was first articulated 24 centuries ago by Epicurus in ancient Greece. Ever since, holy men have twisted themselves into pretzels trying to concoct rebuttals that hold water, but they all leak. A successful rebuttal is impossible. Instead of trying to warp reality to fit theology, a wise person concludes that there is only one believable answer: An all-loving, all-powerful father-creator cannot exist. Nature alone wrought the world's evils.

Christianity is illogical in various other ways. Consider these:

-- The bewildering dogma of the Trinity says father, son and holy ghost are separate, yet the same being, and all three have existed eternally. Does this mean that Jesus impregnated his own virgin mother, causing himself to be born?

-- Homo sapiens sapiens has existed in fully modern form for perhaps 100,000 years, more than 3,000 generations. But Christianity has existed only 2,000 years. Some churches say Jesus is the only conduit to heaven. So what happened to the 2,940 generations of people who died in the preceding 98,000 years? Posthumously, were the "saved" among them declared retroactive Christians?

-- Hundreds of past gods and religions have vanished - such as the Aztec faith, whose priests sacrificed victims to an invisible feathered serpent. Are Christianity's three gods (or one) less perishable?

-- Many Christian end-of-the-world predictions - including a 2011 one by an American evangelist - proved false. New predictions undoubtedly will emerge, and be just as silly.

-- No scientific evidence supports any of the church's miracle claims. The only supposed proofs are ancient writings similar to mythology tales.

-- It's often asserted that Christianity makes people better. If so, why do hundreds of priests and evangelists molest children and commit other "black-collar crimes"? And why did believers inflict centuries of faith-based killings in Crusades, witch hunts, the Inquisition, Reformation wars, pogroms against Jews, drowning of Anabaptists, etc.?

-- Most of the brightest thinkers throughout Western history - philosophers, scientists, writers, democracy reformers and other "greats" - have doubted the church's supernatural claims. Current skeptics stand alongside those towering minds.

In the face of such evidence, why does much of humanity still believe in a father-god? Sigmund Freud saw a clear explanation, as follows:

Tiny tots see a huge father looming over them, loving them, punishing them, protecting them. The image embeds in the infantile subconscious. Years later, when their biological father has lost his awesome majesty, they're told that an invisible, divine father looms over them, loving them, punishing them, protecting them. Bingo - the buried subconscious image makes the god claim seems true.

"The god-creator is openly called Father," Freud wrote. "Psychoanalysis concludes that he really is the father, clothed in the grandeur in which he once appeared to the small child. The religious man... looks back on the memory-image of the overrated father of his childhood, exalts it into a deity, and brings it into the present and into reality. The emotional strength of this memory-image and the lasting nature of his need for protection are the two supports for his belief in God."[3]

When all evidence and knowledge are tallied, thinking people should reach the inevitable conclusion that all gods, devils, heavens, hells, angels, demons, miracles, saviors and other supernatural entities are just fairy tales - fantasies that grew in the fertile human imagination.

1. Alfred Lord Tennyson, *In Memoriam A.H.H.* (1850)

2. Mark Twain, *Letters From the Earth*, Perennial Library, 1974, p. 13

3, Sigmund Freud, *New Introductory Lectures in Psychoanalysis*, 1933

(Written for a proposed book edited by John W. Loftus. Printed in *Freethought Today*, May 2012)

Chapter 23

STATES OF FAITH

Freedom of religion means that the government can't tell you what to believe. Each person is free to reach an individual conclusion about faith.

Every skeptic knows that America's wise founders saw that mixing religion with government power had caused centuries of European horror - so they launched a historic breakthrough, a new advance for civilization: the separation of church and state. Government was forbidden to enforce religion. This safeguard was locked into the First Amendment of the Bill of Rights.

However, some politicians know they can win church votes if they champion government-backed religion. They constantly try to insert sacred claims into public policy. It happened in the 1950s - at the height of the Cold War against "godless communism" - when Congress adopted "In God We Trust" as America's motto and stuck "under God" in the Pledge of Allegiance.

143

These actions clearly violate the separation of church and state. But federal courts pretend that they aren't religious, and therefore are allowable.

Legal challenges against the motto and the pledge produced court decisions calling the affirmations mere "ceremonial deism" that have "lost through rote repletion any significant religious content." One ruling declared that the motto "is of patriotic or ceremonial character and bears no true resemblance to a governmental sponsorship of a religious exercise." But honest people see through this whitewash and recognize that the motto and pledge are unconstitutional government endorsements of religion.

Meanwhile, the problem actually is 50 times worse. All 50 states added holy preambles to their state constitutions. Here are some examples:

Illinois declares that it is "grateful to Almighty God for the civil, political and religious liberty which He hath so long permitted us to enjoy and looking to Him for a blessing on our endeavors."

Maine says it adopted its constitution "acknowledging with grateful hearts the goodness of the Sovereign Ruler of the Universe."

Georgia says it is "relying upon protection and guidance of Almighty God."

Colorado declares "profound reverence for the Supreme Ruler of the Universe."

North Carolina says it is "grateful to Almighty God, the Sovereign Ruler of Nations."

Vermont praises "blessings which the Author

of Existence has bestowed on man."

My own state says: "Since through Divine Providence we enjoy the blessings of civil, political and religious liberty, we the people of West Virginia... reaffirm our faith in and constant reliance upon God."

Etc., etc., etc.

Every state in America thumbs its nose at the separation of church and state.

As far as I can learn, no court challenges have been filed against these brazen violations of the First Amendment.

Maybe secular humanists should launch a nationwide campaign, filing a challenge in every state. If federal courts try to pretend that the holy preambles aren't religious, it would provide a good horselaugh for America and the world.

(from *Free Inquiry*, June-July 2014)

Chapter 24

MY GOD, HOW THE MONEY ROLLS IN

A jobless West Virginian, living on welfare, began preaching in Pentecostal tabernacles to support his family. Within a few years, T.D. Jakes had raked in so much money from believers that he was able to pay $870,000 for two side-by-side mansions, one with a pool and bowling alley. Then his soaring cash flow enabled him to pay $3.2 million for a Texas megachurch vacated by a crooked evangelist who went to prison. Before long, Jakes was grossing more than $20 million annually. Today, he ranks among America's flagrantly rich preachers, traveling by private jet, wearing enormous diamonds, living like royalty.

Thirty-two centuries ago, during the reign of Ramses III, Egypt's great temple of the supreme god Amun-Re - supposed creator of the world and father of the pharaoh - owned 420,000 head of livestock, 65 villages, 83 ships, 433 orchards, vast farmland, and 81,000 workers, all obeying the ruler priests.

In medieval Europe, as the church acquired tighter control over all facets of life, a gold mine was discovered by the clergy. It was simony, the sale of blessings. Fees for absolution, baptism, burial, marriage, etc., escalated into a cash-and-carry system including sale of high church office. Most outrageous were indulgences, church documents bought by worried families to release dead relatives from the alleged pain of an invisible purgatory. In the 1200s, Pope Innocent III denounced simony, saying the clergy "are enthralled to avarice, love presents, and seek rewards; for the sake of bribes they pronounce the godless righteous."

In every age, in almost every culture, priestcraft has been a ticket to comfort. Churches and holy men reap earnings and exalted status from the supernaturalism they administer to followers. As self-proclaimed emissaries of invisible spirits, they outrank common folk, who support them.

The Internal Revenue Service says Americans took tax exemptions for $88 billion in religious donations in 2004 - thus the U.S. Treasury funded churches by forgoing taxes on the $88 billion. And this total doesn't count unknowable sums dropped into Sunday collection plates. Religion is lucrative.

In 1931, amid the misery of the Great Depression, novelist Theodore Dreiser called the church and clergy parasites sponging off people - hypocrites railing against "sin" while doing little for the hungry. "For it is not men who are talking, as they assert, but God through them," Dreiser wrote in Tragic America, "and so through the mouths of tricksters and social prestidigitators, and no more and no less, comes all this hooey in regard to the hereafter." Two centuries earlier, in The Age of Reason, Thomas Paine likewise wrote that religions are "no other than human inventions, set up to terrify and enslave mankind, and monopolize power and profit."

Through the years, other writers have sounded similar warnings. Yet most people rarely think about the giant earnings from faith, or their consequences. The topic mostly escapes notice.

For example, how many know that riches from religion contributed to the downfall of Classical Greece? Few have heard of the Sacred Wars that helped deliver the peninsula into the hands of Alexander the Great. Here's the historical account:

In Ancient Greece, priests reaped wealth through various methods. One apparently was sacred prostitution. The Greek historian-philosopher-geographer Strabo wrote that Corinth's Aphrodite temple had 1,000 consecrated women who served male worshipers for fees, enriching the temple. Presumably the holy hookers were slave women, visited especially by sailors arriving at the large Corinth seaport. If Strabo's account is accurate, religion spawned a profitable bordello.

Even more lucrative were oracles, the fortune-tellers who captivated the ancient world. Superstitious Greeks flocked to oracles. First the worshipers purified themselves by bathing and prayer; then they paid dearly to hear mumbo-jumbo from priests and priestesses.

At Dodona, a barefoot priestess sat in a high cliff, listening to the supposed voice of Zeus in the rustle of leaves or the flutter of dove wings. She provided yes-or-no answers to written questions. At Delphi (named for a dolphin that Apollo allegedly became) a stuporous priestess breathed vapors in a grotto and made incoherent answers, which were "translated" by a priest. The messages were murky - but swallowed avidly by paying believers.

As the fame of the Delphi shrine spread, so did its storehouse of gold, silver and jewels taken from gullible clients. Kings and generals came to Delphi, seeking Apollo's guidance on important decisions, and they brought rich donations to the gods. Soon, various city-states built treasuries around the shrine to hold the wealth. The Amphictyonic League, a consortium of twelve city-states including Athens and Sparta, governed Delphi cooperatively and secured its riches, like directors of a bank.

But money breeds trouble. Mountain people surrounding the shrine, the Phocians, saw an opportunity to cash in on the holy traffic, and began levying steep fees on visitors. Other members of the League sent troops to halt the extra profiteering. Phocians resisted. The First Sacred War erupted in 601 BCE and lasted 10 years. The Phocians were defeated and forced to serve the shrine.

A century later, in 480 BCE, a Persian army under Xerxes marched on Delphi to seize its wealth, but a landslide (caused by Apollo, the faithful said) blocked the troops.

A generation later, Phocians again grabbed Delphi's treasuries, and the Amphictyonic League again attacked. This Second Sacred War, in 447 BCE, ended like the first.

Seventy years later, a different stash of religious wealth was looted. During many, many wars between Greek city-states, an Arcadian army plundered treasuries of the mighty temple of Zeus at Olympia in southwest Greece. Naturally, this theft triggered more warring by kings and assemblies who had donated riches to the Supreme God.

Soon afterward, back at Delphi, the Third Sacred War flared in 356 BCE when Phocians seized the Apollo shrine once more. Phocian leaders promised not to loot the treasuries - but soon did so. The wealth that had been drained from believers was squandered to hire mercenary soldiers to battle neighbors, to bribe opposing generals, and to reward cronies. Historian Charles Morris related:

"One hundred seventeen ingots of gold and 360 golden goblets went to the melting pot, and with them a golden statue three cubits high, and a lion of the same precious metal. And what added to the horror of pious Greece was that much of the proceeds of these treasures was lavished on favorites. Necklaces of Helen and Eriphyle were given to dissolute women, and a woman flute-player received a silver cup and a golden wreath from the temple hoard."

This time, the Amphictyonic League had been sadly weakened by centuries of fighting, especially by the Peloponnesian War between Athens and Sparta, and by constant conflict with Persia. From the north, King Philip of Macedonia had been gaining power, expanding his territory, and sending legions in attempts to grab Greek lands. After the Delphi shrine was seized a third time, some local assemblies asked Philip to drive out the occupying Phocians. Shrewdly, he obliged. Posing as devoted champion of Apollo, he waged a long war that finally quelled the temple-grabbers. To inflict the vengeance of the god upon the looters, Philip drowned 3,000 Phocian prisoners on charges of sacrilege. Subtly, he formed Greek "alliances" that made him de facto ruler and protector of the holies.

Then the Fourth Sacred War erupted in 339 after a different neighbor state invaded the sanctified Delphi region. The Amphictyonic League asked the Macedonian army to save the oracle temple again. However, some city-states perceived that Philip was using his defense of Apollo as a pretext to seize large sections of the peninsula. They fielded troops to resist - but ten thousand Macedonians in full battle array were unstoppable. At a crucial clash at Chaeronea, Philip's army crushed Athens, Thebes and other allies. Philip's son, Alexander - who had been born at the start of the Third Sacred War - was a brilliant 18-year-old cavalry commander in the decisive massacre.

Victory in the Fourth Sacred War gave Philip complete control of Greece, except for defiant Sparta in the south. But he didn't live to rule. He was assassinated in 336 by a crazed guard, and Alexander took command. Greece was subsumed beneath Macedonia in a mighty war machine, an engine of conquest. The era of city-states ended. After Alexander's death, Greece fell under Roman rule. More than 2,000 years were to pass before it regained independence.

Although Ancient Greece had multitudes of wars, and plenty of other self-destructive factors, wealth taken by priests from the gullible was a trigger that helped topple the classic civilization.

It's a little-known footnote in the age-old tale of riches from religion. Apparently, the tale never will end, as long as believers feel compelled to give tribute to purveyors of the supernatural.

(from *Free Inquiry*, Dec-Jan 2006-07)

Chapter 25

THE STORY BEHIND WACO'S TRAGEDY

Most Americans remember the historic 1993 siege of the Branch Davidian cult compound at Waco, Texas, which left eighty cultists and four federal officers dead. But did you know that the story actually began 150 years ago with a famous fiasco?

Since watching weird religion is my hobby, I'll tell you the tale:

In the 1830s, a New England Baptist preacher, William Miller, computed from obscure prophecies in the Book of Daniel that Jesus would return to Earth between March 21, 1843, and March 21, 1844. Miller began warning of the approaching apocalypse. By the 1840s, he had drawn nearly 100,000 followers.

When the fateful time arrived, the "Millerites" prayed and prayed - but nothing happened. Then Miller re-examined the Bible verses and announced that he had erred; the correct date would be Oct. 22, 1844. As it neared, many of the faithful gave away their possessions and waited on hilltops for the heavens to open. Again, zilch.

Many Millerites lost their faith, but a hard core held firm. Some of them insisted that doomsday actually had occurred on Oct. 22, but it was a preparatory event in heaven that would be followed soon by Jesus bursting forth onto Earth. This group formed the Seventh-day Adventist Church.

As the Seventh-day Adventists grew more than 3 million strong, some members felt that the church wasn't holy enough. In the 1930s, a Los Angeles Adventist, Victor Houteff, said Jesus wouldn't return until an ultra-pure church was ready to greet him. So Houteff opened a Waco commune for pure believers, calling them Davidian Seventh-day Adventists.

He died in 1955, and the Davidians prayerfully awaited his resurrection. When it didn't happen, his widow Florence took over. She proclaimed that the Second Coming would be on Easter Day, 1959. Hundreds of followers around America quit their jobs, sold their belongings, and hurried to Waco for the rapture. Wrong again.

Once more, the disillusioned departed, and a hard core persisted. A member named Ben Roden took command and named the survivors Branch Davidians. He died in 1978, leaving the commune, called Mount Carmel, to his widow Lois and son George.

Soon afterward, a 23-year-old Texas Adventist named Vernon Howell, a ninth-grade dropout, moved into the compound (and reportedly became the lover of the 67-year-old widow). He had hypnotic charisma, electrifying the others with his revelations of the coming apocalypse.

He married the 14-year-old daughter of a commune couple - but soon declared that God had commanded him to establish a House of David, in which he was to have as many wives as King David. He bedded more than a dozen commune females, one merely 11, another 50. He gave each a Star of David to wear as an emblem that she had been chosen by the king.

After Lois Roden died in 1986, her son George vied with Howell for command. Roden won, temporarily. Howell took his followers and left Mount Carmel, wandering as nomads. Then in 1987, Howell's band returned to challenge Roden for leadership.

Roden proposed an epic contest: From a graveyard, he dug up the corpse of an 85-year-old woman, and declared that whoever could resurrect her would be the true prophet of Mount Carmel. Howell evaded, and urged police to arrest Roden for corpse abuse.

Then Howell and seven armed supporters crept into Mount Carmel in after-midnight darkness. Roden grabbed his Uzi machine gun and engaged the intruders in a firefight. He was wounded slightly in the hand and chest. Howell's band was charged with attempted murder, and released on bond.

Next, Roden was jailed for contempt of court because he filed grossly obscene motions in an unrelated case. While Roden was locked up, Howell moved his followers back into the compound and took over.

Their subsequent trial for attempted murder ended in acquittals. The dethroned Roden later killed a man and was put in a state mental hospital.

Reigning as sole prophet, Howell preached that he was an angel sent by God to implement the Second Coming. He said God ordained him to move to Israel and convert the Jews, which would trigger the Battle of Armageddon and make Earth a paradise for the surviving faithful. Howell visited Israel - but failed to convert the Jews.

Traveling around the globe, the dynamic young prophet attracted converts who sold their possessions, gave all their money to him, and followed him to Waco to live in the compound. In 1989, he proclaimed that all women in the compound were his brides, and the rest of the men must remain celibate. Some married couples rebelled and left. Others, utterly dominated by him, obeyed.

In 1990, Howell changed his name to David Koresh and began preaching that the great doomsday battle would occur in Texas. He and his lieutenants bought hundreds of guns and machine guns, plus ammunition, plus gas masks and other war supplies.

Federal agents heard that the commune contained illegal machine guns, and took steps to disarm the cult. The siege and its outcome are a well-known American tragedy. Surrounded zealots allowed themselves and their children to burn to death, rather than walk out to safety.

The Waco saga has entered history, like Jonestown, the witch-hunts and other bizarre episodes. As we go about our daily lives, it's unsettling to realize that some people among us are capable of believing far-out fantasies, enough even to die for them.

(from *Free Inquiry* - Summer 1994)

Chapter 26

THE DREAMS THAT STUFF IS MADE OF

The European Southern Observatory - a 15-nation consortium that operates telescopes in Chile - recently released a photo of two galaxies colliding. Here's the stunner: It happened 7 billion years ago, when the universe was younger, but it took 7 billion years for fast-traveling light to reach Planet Earth just now. To look at the image today is looking backward in time through incredible eons.

If you follow science, you may get an eerie sense that daily reality - people, houses, cars, trees, air, earth and all the rest - is just a shred amid a hugely greater array of existence. Philosopher-engineer R. Buckminster Fuller put it this way:

"Up to the 20th century, 'reality' was everything humans could touch, smell, see and hear. Since the initial publication of the chart of the electromagnetic spectrum, humans have learned that what they can touch, smell, see and hear is less than one-millionth of reality."

Here are some random examples:

Each cell of your body (except red blood cells) has about six feet of DNA tightly coiled into 46 chromosomes in its nucleus. Since the human body has an estimated 37 trillion cells, each person contains perhaps 30 billion miles of DNA.

When you sit perfectly "still," you're traveling vastly faster than a bullet - 1,000 miles per hour with Earth's rotation (at the equator), 67,000 mph with the planet's orbit around the sun, 486,000 mph with the solar system's whirl around the Milky Way galaxy, and an estimated 1.3 million mph with the galaxy's travel through the universe. A bullet goes about 3,000 mph.

When electrons come loose from atoms, they can make spectacular lightning or the current flow driving the entire modern electrical age. In most atoms, electrons are placid because they're paired in couples of opposite "spin" (which doesn't mean whirling). But iron atoms have a few electrons that aren't paired, making each atom a magnet. When all the atoms in a piece of iron become aligned, it creates a magnet powerful enough to make maglev (magnetic levitation) trains hover above rails. The spin of electrons is more powerful than gravity.

Einstein's relativity is fully accepted today. But ask yourself: Can time really slow down and dimensions shorten as speed increases?

Einstein's famed $E=MC^2$ equation showed that matter and energy are interchangeable. Less matter than a dime turned into energy at Hiroshima in 1945.

Nobody really knows what subatomic particles are. Sometimes they're objects; sometimes they're waves. They seemingly exist in several places at once. They're "the dreams that stuff is made of," one physicist said. Some "virtual particles" appear and vanish in pure vacuum.

Physicists Paul Davies and John Gribbin wrote a book titled *The Matter Myth*, which contends that "materialism is dead." Quote:

"Quantum physics undermines materialism because it reveals that matter has far less substance than we might believe.... An extension of quantum theory, known as quantum field theory... paints a picture in which solid matter dissolves away, to be replaced by weird excitations and vibrations of invisible field energy. In this theory, little distinction remains between material substance and apparently empty space, which itself seethes with ephemeral quantum activity."

Here's a grabber: Nearly all the weight, or mass, of matter comes from protons and neutrons, which are composed of three quarks each. Yet the masses of three quarks add up to just one percent of the mass of a proton or neutron. *NewScientist* says theorists think that actions of the strong nuclear force, which binds quarks together, creates 99 percent of the mass.

Atoms are as empty as the night sky. If one were as big as a cathedral, its nucleus would be the size of a grain of salt. Yet these voids form solid-seeming matter, because their negative outer electrons repel each other.

When emptiness is squeezed from atoms - when intense gravity compresses a collapsing

160

star into a pulsar, a solid mass of neutrons - the substance weighs 10 million tons per thimbleful. Astounding.

To show the mysteries of existence, California Unitarian minister Ted Webb cited statistics like these:

"Your body and mine make 300 million new cells every minute."

"The information in the DNA molecule in every cell would fill a thousand 600-page books."

What conclusion can be drawn from all this? Here's mine: Science shows that reality is amazing, baffling, incredible, bizarre, seemingly miraculous. I can't imagine why anyone would need supernatural gods, devils, heavens and hells of religion - purely fictitious, as far as any honest observer can learn - when science reveals greater enigmas.

(from *Free Inquiry* - Dec.-Jan. 2014-15)

Chapter 27

NO QUALMS

I'm quite aware that my turn is approaching. The realization hovers in my mind like a frequent companion.

My wife died five years ago. Dozens, hundreds, of my longtime friends and colleagues likewise came to the end of their journeys. They number so many that I keep a "Gone" list in my computer to help me remember them all. Before long, it will be my turn to join the list.

I'm 81 and still work full-time. I feel keen and eager for life. My hair's still dark (mostly). I have a passel of children, grandchildren and rambunctious great-grandchildren. I love sailing my beloved dinghy on our small private lake, and hiking in shady forests with my three-legged dog, and taking a gifted grandson to symphony, and seeking wisdom in our long-running Unitarian philosophy-and-science circle. I now live with an adorable woman in her 70s, and we relish our togetherness. But her health is fragile. Her turn is on the horizon too.

I have no dread. Why worry about the inescapable, the utterly unavoidable, the sure destiny of today's seven billion? However, sometimes I feel annoyed because I will have no choice. I'm accustomed to choosing whatever course I want - but I won't get to decide whether to take my final step. Damn!

I have no supernatural beliefs. I don't expect to wake up in Paradise or Hades, surrounded by angels or demons. That's fairy-tale stuff. I think my personality, my identity - me - is created by my brain, and when the brain dies, so does the psyche. Gone forever into oblivion.

I'll admit that some reports of "near-death experiences" raise tantalizing speculation about a hereafter. But, in the end, I assume those blinding lights and out-of-body flotations are just final glimmers from oxygen deprivation. I guess I'll find out soon enough.

It takes courage to look death in the eye and feel ready. Sobeit. Bring it on. I won't flinch. Do your damnedest. I'll never whimper. However, maybe this is bluster and bravado, an attempt to feel strong in the face of what will happen regardless of how I react.

Unlike Dylan Thomas, I won't rage, rage against the dying of the light. Instead, I plan to live as intensely as I can, while I can, and then accept the inevitable. I find solace in wisdom I've heard from other departees. Just before she died of ovarian cancer, one of my longtime friends, Marty Wilson, wrote:

"I often think of humankind as a long procession whose beginning and end are out of sight. We the living... have no control over when or where we enter the procession, or even how long we are part of it, but we do get to choose our marching companions. And we can all exercise some control over what direction the procession takes, what part we play, and how we play it."

In *The Fire Next Time*, brilliant writer James Baldwin said:

"Life is tragic simply because the earth turns and the sun inexorably rises and sets, and one day, for each of us, the sun will go down for the last, last time. Perhaps the root of our trouble, the human trouble, is that we will sacrifice all the beauty of our lives, will imprison ourselves in totems, taboos, crosses, blood sacrifices, steeples, mosques, races, armies, flags, nations, in order to deny the fact of death, which is the only fact we have."

Legendary lawyer Clarence Darrow, wrote:

"When we fully understand the brevity of life, its fleeting joys and unavoidable pains; when we accept the fact that all men and women are approaching an inevitable doom; the consciousness of it should make us more kindly and considerate of each other. This feeling should make men and women use their best efforts to help their fellow travelers on the road, to make the path brighter and easier... for the wayfarers who must live a common life and die a common death."

My journey on the road has been proceeding for eight decades. Actuarial tables make my future so obvious that I can't shut my eyes to it. Life proceeds through stages, and I'm in the last scene of the last act.

I have a Pantheon of my favorite heroes: Einstein, Jefferson, Voltaire, Lincoln, Carl Sagan, Shakespeare, Martin Luther King Jr., Tolstoy, FDR, Beethoven, Epicurus, Gandhi, etc. They fill a different "Gone" list. They uplifted humanity, even transformed humanity, in their day - but their day ended, and life moved on.

My day was the 1960s, and '70s, and '80s, even the '90s. I was a Whirling Dervish in the thick of everything. Life was a fascinating carnival. But it slides into the past so deftly you hardly notice.

While my clock ticks away, I'll pursue every minute. Carpe diem. Make hay while the sun shines. And then I'm ready for nature's blackout, with no regrets.

(from *Free Inquiry*, Oct.-Nov. 2013 - and *Charleston Sunday Gazette-Mail*, Sept. 22, 2013)

Previous books by
James A. Haught

Holy Horrors: An Illustrated History of Religious Murder and Madness - (Prometheus Books, 1990). Translated into Spanish as *Horror Sagrado*, Turkish as *Kutsal Dehpet*, Portuguese as *Persguicoes Religiosas*, and Polish as *Swiety Koszmar*.

Science in a Nanosecond: Illustrated Answers to 100 Basic Science Questions - (Prometheus, 1990). Translated into Polish as *Nauka w Nanosekunde* and Italian as *Il Vuoto di Torricelli*.

The Art of Lovemaking: An Illustrated Tribute - (Prometheus, 1992). A gallery of lovers by major artists, showing the beauty of sex, countering both church taboos and the crudity of pornographers.

Holy Hatred: Religious Conflicts of the '90s - (Prometheus, 1995). Translated into Japanese by Jiji Press, 1996, and into Turkish as *Kutsal Nephret*.

2,000 Years of Disbelief: Famous People With the Courage to Doubt - (Prometheus, 1996).

Holy Horrors (expanded paperback after 9/11) - (Prometheus, 2002).

Honest Doubt: Essays on Atheism in a Believing Society - (Prometheus, 2007).

Amazon Moon, a freethought novel of fabled women warriors, citing religious sacrifices, oracles and Sacred Wars in ancient Greece - (BookLocker, 2007).

Fascinating West Virginia: Wild, Memorable Episodes From the Longtime Editor of the Mountain State's Largest Newspaper - (Charleston Gazette, 2008)

Fading Faith: The Rise of the Secular Age - (Gustav Broukal Press, 2010)

BIOGRAPHY

James A. Haught was born in 1932 in a small West Virginia farm town that had no electricity or paved streets. He graduated from a rural high school with 13 students in the senior class. He came to Charleston, worked as a delivery boy, then became a teen-age apprentice printer at the *Charleston Daily Mail* in 1951. Developing a yen to be a reporter, he volunteered to work without pay in the *Daily Mail* newsroom on his days off, to learn the trade. This arrangement continued several months, until *The Charleston Gazette* offered a full-time news job in 1953. He has been at the Gazette ever since - except for a few months in 1959 when he was press aide to Sen. Robert Byrd.

During his half-century in newspaper life, he has been police reporter, religion columnist, feature writer and night city editor - then he was investigative reporter for 13 years, and his work led to several corruption convictions. In 1983 he was named associate editor, and in 1992 he became editor. He writes nearly 400 Gazette editorials a year, plus occasional personal columns and news articles.

Haught has won 21 national newswriting awards, and is author of ten books and 85 national magazine articles. Thirty of his columns have been distributed by national syndicates. He also is a senior editor of *Free Inquiry* magazine. He is listed in *Who's Who in America* and *Contemporary Authors*. He has four children, 12 grandchildren and eight great-grandchildren.

Personally, he enjoys hiking with a trail club, participating in a philosophy group, and taking grandchildren swimming off his old sailboat. He is a longtime member of Charleston's Unitarian Universalist Congregation.

17792247R00106

Made in the USA
San Bernardino, CA
17 December 2014